# From My Window
## and other poems

*Yvonne Hollenbeck*

*Poetry and Stories of the American West*

*From My Window*
© 2005 Yvonne Hollenbeck

ISBN: 1-57579-321-0

Library of Congress Control Number: 2005909786

To contact the author or order copies, contact:

Yvonne Hollenbeck
30549 291st Street
Clearfield SD 57580
605-557-3559
geetwo@gwtc.net
www.hollenbeck.com.

*Printed in the United States of America*
PINE HILL PRESS
4000 West 57th Street
Sioux Falls, SD 57106

*To my grandchildren*

# Acknowledgments

I wish to thank the following people who shared
their memories and photographs with me for
use in this book:

*Syble Brown*
*Jeri L. Dobrowski (cover prairie and windmill photo)*
*Harry and Ruth Hanson*
*Dema Hollenbeck*
*Elaine Kayton*
*Vern and Viola Keszler*
*Betty Littau*
*Scott Nelson*
*Russ and June Sorenson*
*Billie Synder Thornburg*


and a special thanks to the following people
for their help and encouragement:

*Margo Metegrano*
*Pat Richardson*
*Red Steagall*


and to my husband, *Glen Hollenbeck,*
for not only his help and encouragement,
but for being such a good sport when
I write poems (true or not) about him;

and

to *CowboyPoetry.com* for all their
support and promotion, not only of me,
but of all the folks involved with the
western entertainment and
cowboy poetry business.

# From My Window

From my window I can see the first dim light of day
and the cowboys, saddled up, are headed out;
they'll be rounding up the cattle, for it's branding time again,
and their favorite time of year, without a doubt.

By week's end they'll be riding in, their job will be complete
and I'll see 'em top that far and distant hill;
from my window I'll be watching as they head their horses home,
and to see this is a special kind of thrill.

Not even Charlie Russell, with a paint brush in his hand,
could paint the scenes I see from day to day.
I'm sure a lot of folks may think that this is mighty strange,
but I wouldn't have it any other way.

I get a glimpse of heaven from my window every day,
and I suppose my very favorite thing
is when the winter's finally past and nature bursts anew,
and a meadowlark announces, "it is spring!"

So, hats off to the poets and the singers of the songs,
and the writers for the stories they portray,
as they tell the world about the special life out here
...the way of life I'm blessed to see each day,

from my window.

# Contents

## Life on the Prairie

## Cowboys, Horses and Rodeos

## Holidays on the Range

## Patchwork on the Prairie

# Foreword

This is without a doubt some of Yvonne's finest poetry, and when it come to cowboy poetry, she's as good as any and better than most. The only thing more enjoyable than reading her poetry is listening to her recite it in person. It baffles me how she can connect with a crowd of "cow" people, instantly. I have to come out telling jokes to really hook a crowd, while she saunters out out, waves to the crowd and says, "hi there" and the whole crowd wants to follow her home and eat her homemade bread. She and her husband Glen, who is one of the top Senior Tie Down Ropers in the country, run a cow and calf outfit near Clearfield, South Dakota.

Yvonne has been around cows, horses, and cowboys all her life and lives right smack in the middle of the things she writes about. She knows the good, the bad, and the ugly, but enough about my three brothers. Her poetry runs the gamut from hilariously funny to thought-provoking serious ones that will darn sure make grown cowboys daub at their eyes, hoping no one is watching. People like Yvonne and Baxter Black have a gift that can't be learned. It's the ability to "connect" with people, and it doesn't matter if they've never been close to a cow, or raised with them. It's a common sense approach that leaves you wondering why you never thought of that yourself. It's the real gristle and bone of ranch life from the mind of a great poet.

I've learned a lot from Yvonne and perhaps someday I'll be able to put some of it to good use, but believe me when I tell you: "once you've read her poems, a windmill, yearling colt, or (I hate to admit this) even a bunch of damn flowers on a side hill will never look the same again."

Enjoy the book.

*Pat Richardson*

# Introduction

Between the years 1840 and 1870, a quarter million Americans crossed rugged trails seeking a future in the West. Soon after, settlement started on the Great Plains. In the 1880's, much of Nebraska and the Dakotas were opened to homesteading, the last allotments being offered in the early 1900s in Western Dakota. The last big cattle herds were rounded up and shipped out, thus ending the open range days, and the great Indian tribes were confined to meager reservations.

It was in the 1880's when all of my great grandparents settled in either Nebraska or South Dakota. This period of homesteading produced much evidence that the women did not always welcome the idea of moving to this new frontier, and most endured hardships beyond the imagination. Many left fine homes in the East to establish new homes in tar paper shacks or sod houses on virgin prairie inhabited by predators and rattlesnakes. These people lived in constant fear of prairie fires, Indian uprisings, blizzards and plagues.

As a new life was established, the women were forced to make changes in order to survive. Isolation brought a yearning for the places they had once called home, and there were two things that seemed to help bridge the gap between their new life and the previous one. Those two things were also documented in nearly every journal and historical account on the lives of these pioneer women: the making of quilts and writing poetry. Today, every museum in the Great Plains contains faded quilts and sheets of handwritten poetry as testimony to the lives of those pioneer women.

Many of these pioneer women, my grandmothers included, documented the fact that either writing poetry or making quilts was their link to sanity during a time when life became nearly unbearable. Fortunately, I have been left with a large collection of both, and was not only taught both of these skills, but was greatly influenced by these grandmothers.

Because this book contains stories about these pioneer farm and ranch women, many focusing on the role quilt making had in their lives, as well as poetry that reflects upon my life as a modern day cattleman's wife, I hope the reader can weave the various patterns of the lives set forth on the pages herein in the same manner as my grandmothers wove pieces of cloth into quilts, and words into poetry.

# Life on the Prairie

*I purchased a book called "Western Words" by Ramon F. Adams. It is a dictionary containing over 5,000 words heard in the West. In this dictionary there is not one mention of a ranch wife. In fact, about the only mention of a female is the word "harlot." Needless to say, this upset me to the point that I found myself writing a poem about it.*

# THE "WESTERN WORDS" DICTIONARY

We raise a lot of horses out on our Dakota ranch
    and my husband likes to break some every time he gets a chance.
But there's way too many horses for the time he has, no doubt,
    so we hire extra wranglers to help him break 'em out.

There's a standard protocol, when you live out in the sticks,
    that you feed the men that's working, ...early morning, noon and six.
When these fellers get to talking 'bout the horses during lunch
    I hear the darndest lingo as I listen to that bunch.

Of course, I understand words like saddles, shoes and tack,
    but I hear words like "cayuse, jingling hosses, mars and kack."
It's almost like they're speaking in some distant, foreign tongue;
    so I thought I'd try to learn more 'bout where these words come from.

I went into a bookstore on my monthly trip to town
    and found a Dictionary called: "Western Verbs and Nouns."
I spent twelve hard-earned dollars on that handy little book
    and didn't make it home before I had to have a look.

I found out that a "cayuse" describes a wild horse;
    and "jingling" means to gather horses, which makes sense, of course.
"Kack" is slang for saddle, and you spell it with a "k,"
    but I couldn't find what "mar" meant, and I searched most the day.

But then one day a storm came up, and lightning lit the sky,
   poor Jim Bob came a-running . . .(he's a little Texas guy).
He shouted: "Call for halp 'cause some bolts, they caused a far!"
   It dawned on me that Texans call a female horse is called a "mar."

But one thing got me sideways, as I studied every day
   my little dictionary of the cowboy and his ways.
I had learned that cooks are "coosies" like a "mar" is just a mare,
   but there wasn't any mention of a "ranch wife" anywhere.

Isn't that the berries that they'd leave the ranch wife out
   of a book about the West and what it's all about?
Well, I was hoppin' mad when those guys came in to eat
   and they couldn't seem to figure out why I had burned the meat.

They started talkin' horses with their grammar from the West
   when I slammed that little book down and started to protest
that they forgot the ranch wife when they published that darned book
   and I wondered how they'd like it on the range without a cook!

They all gave me the strangest looks, like I was just a "crab"
   and they still use all that lingo when they sit and eat and gab.
And many days have come and gone but I will not forget
   how I blew twelve hard-earned dollars just to get myself upset!


*and by the way, here is my definition of a ranch wife:*
*"A female who knows how to do everything described in this book!"*

# A RANCH WIFE

I've been asked many times in my travels
what it's like on a ranch in the West;
and I guess that my life is quite different,
'cause there aren't many ranch wives that's left.

I often work hard and sometimes there's tasks
that other gals don't have to do;
and of course I get lonely out there on the range
where neighbors are far and so few.

But views from my windows span many a mile,
and often mirages appear;
I see the sunrise, the pretty sunsets,
and coyote and eagle and deer.

There's never a day that I don't get to see
the wonders of nature abound;
it might be a rainbow, a new baby calf,
or a fresh snow a-covering the ground.

Oh, there's times when I have to go work like a man
doing jobs where there never is pay;
but rewards can be great when you help save a calf
or you've helped with a harvest of hay.

I know lots of women don't have it so hard
but I never would trade 'em my life.
I love my dear cowboy, my home on the range,
and just being a plain ol' ranch wife.

*Mrs. McCance at her daughter, Florry Houk's grave.*

*Florry died following the birth of her firstborn, a baby girl. The baby, named Margie, lived. Florry's sister, Grace Snyder, wrote this account in her biography, "No Time On My Hands:"*

*"We buried Florry from Walnut Grove Church on Sunday and laid her to rest in the pretty cemetery across the road. Poppie had helped set out a young cedar hedge around the burying ground a few years back, and it was surprising how tall it had grown already. Stell took the baby back to the Platte with her, and Ethel and I went on home with John to help put Florry's things away. Among them I found enough pieces, cut and laid in neat piles, for a 'Wild-goose Chase' quilt. I told John I'd take them home with me, and when the baby grew up I'd make them into a quilt for her."*

*Grace McCance Snyder (1882-1982)*

*One hot day in August, I spent several hours helping fight a prairie fire at a neighboring ranch. When I returned home, I was hot, dirty, tired, hungry, thirsty, and crabby. I turned on television to see if there was any chance of rain in the forecast, only to see Martha Stewart showing how to properly iron table linens. As tired as I was, I wrote this poem before I went to bed that night:*

# WHAT WOULD MARTHA DO?

Martha's making millions showing people how to cook
    with her syndicated TV Show, her magazines and books.
But she don't know a darned bit more than gals like me and you
    'though we don't get a nickel for the many things we do.

It never seems to matter when her hair gets in her eyes;
    she just pulls it back and then commences making cakes and pies.
She licks the batter off her fingers right there on TV,
    and why she's getting paid for it sure beats the likes of me.

I wonder if she'd fair so well if she lived on a ranch;
    and what she'd use to get manure off of boots and pants.
And when she's plumb exhausted and she has to feed a crew,
    I sometimes stop and wonder: *"What would Martha do?"*

When hubby hollers that he's stuck and he could use a tow,
    would she know how to find the gears and let the clutch out slow?
I wonder how she'd do sorting yearlings through a gate.
    That would test her many skills . . . perhaps would be her fate.

Would she know how to fix a fence and put a splice in wire,
    or use a soaked-up gunnysack to fight a prairie fire?
When she's using cream and eggs, do you 'spose that she'd know how
    to clean a hen-house, separate, or milk a kicking cow?

Her fancy TV oven, I doubt would fill the bill,
    when in the house he brings a calf that's taken on a chill.
Would she know how to do the chores when hubby has the flu?
    I sometimes stop and wonder: *"What would Martha do?"*

Last week I helped with fencing . . . we went for quite a ways;
  I hadn't done my housework in more than several days.
I came home sore and tired, and much to my surprise
  were a couple cattle buyers, so I had to feed those guys.

And then I set another plate, 'cause guess who next arrived;
  the banker, with his briefcase, came pulling in our drive.
He said that he was passing by, so thought he'd stop and look
  at our cattle and our horses and he'd like to check my books.

Now folks, I'd been real busy, and my books were way behind,
  but I told him he could check them . . . I really didn't mind,
'cause the records that I showed him were far from being true.
  After all, I got to thinking: *"What would Martha do?"*

Illustration by Scott Nelson; Solen, North Dakota

# WHY JANE LEFT TED

I'm sure you've seen the tabloids
   ...don't believe a thing they've said;
I think I know the real scoop
   as to just why Jane left Ted.
This was overheard in Thedford
   by a coffee drinking crew;
by the time it got to my house,
   you can bet the story's true.

They said Jane was getting restless,
   her life was just a bore;
with all her wealth and luxury,
   she wanted something more.
So, Ted with all his billions
   thought he'd give her back her life
and thought just what she needed
   was to be a rancher's wife.

He'd seen 'em in the movies
   in their homes out on the range,
and thought that his dear Janie
   could use this kind of change.
He bought a bunch of ranches,
   put together quite a spread;
the "biggest rancher in the West!"
   At least that's what they said.

He stocked his range with buffalo,
   red fox, and prairie dogs;
to heck with raisin' cattle,
   sheep, or horses, corn and hogs.
His jet brought her to Omaha
   (the place her dad called home)
from there they drove the Hummer
   out to where his bison roam.

8

And just like every rancher does
    when driving with their mates,
they only do the driving
    while the ranch wife gets the gates!
In spite of her aerobics,
    her body was not fit
for a ranch of fifty townships
    and all its gates to git!

Jet lag mixed with blisters,
    by the time they made their house
had started causing stress upon
    this wealthy rancher's spouse.
The next day was pure hell on earth,
    at least that's what she said
...the day the cookie crumbled
    and the reason Jane left Ted.

'Cause what she hadn't planned on,
    something city gals don't do,
she had to rise at 5 a.m.
    and feed a ranch hand crew.
Ted said to be a rancher's wife
    she had to look the part;
he handed her an old wool cap
    and tattered old carharts.

Next came yellow work gloves,
    then knee-high rubber boots;
he showed her where the buckets were,
    the log chains, and the scoops.
And on that frosty morning
    when she'd plan to sleep in late,
he had her in the muck and mud
    sorting bison through a gate!

Do you 'spose that bison prolapse?
    Did she have to lance a cyst?
Did they vaccinate for BVD
    as the neighbors would insist?
No one knows what happened,
    at least no one will say,
but she went back to Georgia,
    and left poor Ted that day.

They claim the West is hell on horses,
    hell on women too;
the breakup of this marriage
    is just proof that theory's true.
She said to be a rancher's wife,
    she'd rather be caught dead;
and now you know the truth about
    the reason Jane left Ted.

This early-day sod house was located in the Nebraska
Sandhills where many of Ted's bison now roam.

# THE CORNER GROCERY STORE

They say she almost crumbled when he told her he was through;
he wanted to be free again . . . he'd found somebody new.

She thought about their wedding day and when they bought the ranch;
how hard she'd worked; now it's through, she wished she had a chance

to win again his tender love, but Wilbur said "no more!"
and Molly's bucking fifty . . . the new chick's twenty-four.

Her heart was nearly broken as Molly went that day
to buy some feed and vaccine and to see about some hay.

She knew that he'd be moved out by the time she got back home;
and it'd be tough to knuckle down and run the ranch alone.

The last stop was for taters at the Corner Grocery Store;
the world was on her shoulders; how could she take much more.

But Lady Luck was on her side (she didn't know it then).
She only had one dollar left when, what the hell, she'd spend

it on the high stakes lotto, and much to her delight,
the numbers that were later drawn matched her card that night.

When Wilbur heard of Molly's luck, he headed for the ranch;
he said he was mistaken and would like another chance.

The girlfriend he'd left with didn't look too good no more;
but Molly didn't buy it as she showed the jerk the door!

Now Molly's still a-ranching and has bought a couple more.
Poor Wilbur's sacking groceries at the Corner Grocery Store!

*My husband's maternal grandmother, Jennie McMurtry, wrote articles in various newspapers under the pen name of "Nebraska Jane." This is an article she wrote about hunting rattlesnakes. She lived in a sod house on what was called "Buffalo Flats" in Brown County, Nebraska. Rattlesnakes were plentiful in that area.*

# SNAKES
### by Jennie McMurtry (1898-1946)

Suppose you were to hear someone say, "We are going snake hunting this afternoon. Want to go along?"

Would you think they were planning some jungle expedition?

You might hear that if you were visiting me, here in the edge of the Nebraska Sandhills. And the snakes are about as poisonous as those found anywhere. Quite often on a warm Sunday afternoon in early spring or late fall, someone will get together a bunch and go over to the rattlesnake dens to hunt snakes. These are good sized holes in the sunny slope of a white-looking cliff, which is dotted here and there with stunted evergreen trees. Here the snakes hole up for winter, but leave the dens during the summer and scatter for miles over the country. On warm days in spring and fall, they lay around the openings of the dens and sun themselves.

Upon arriving at the cliff, we can see nothing of them, but don't be so foolish as to try to climb down there. The men see to their rifles and now one of them picks up a small rock and tosses it down the bluff when it lands with a "thud." Instantly we see a movement, and one ugly head after another rears in the air, and there is a continual buzz of rattles. The men take careful aim and pick them off, one after another. Thirty-seven were killed on one afternoon recently.

It is not only excitement and sport for the men but also a great good to the community to get rid of those dangerous reptiles, as much livestock is lost, cattle and dogs especially, and sometimes a horse, from their poisonous bite. And there would be more human lives lost if it were not for that quick transportation, and good medical care are almost always available.

/s/ Nebraska Jane

Mrs. W. L. McMurtry – Ainsworth, Nebraska

Herbert and Edwin Sachtjen, homesteaders appproximately six miles North of our ranch, and their team that were bit by rattlesnakes one day when they were nearly done putting up hay.

This is the same team prior to their encounter with rattlesnakes.

*Written at the request of Jim Thompson and Francie Ganje of Creative Broadcast Services in Spearfish, South Dakota, during Cowboy Poetry Week, 2005.*

# QUEEN OF THE COW TOWNS

Out in Western South Dakota on the North edge of the hills
    lies a bit of paradise there on the plain.
It's a pretty town named "Spearfish," born in 1876,
    and it seemed that every cowman praised her name.

The hills were filled with miners who had come to search for gold
    but the gold they found was not beneath the ground;
soon a million head of cattle would be grazing in her fold
    on grasslands besting any gold they'd found.

Now folks, a lot of cow towns have sprung up across the land,
    since the coming of the cattle to the range;
but with them came the wire, the wagons and the rails,
    and a lot of them could not withstand the change.

But not this grand ol' lady, she'd withstand the test of time;
    it's been proven by her deeds and not her words.
She played host to the roundups, to the cowboys and their camps
    and they found her arms wide open to their herds.

But the blacksmith forged a new day, and the roundups are all through,
    though you still can hear the echoes of their sound;
and the cowboys, oh the cowboys...their spirit's in her valleys,
    and their trails are but a shadow on the ground.

And though we've seen the changes since the days of long ago,
    her beauty's still a notch above the rest.
That prairie town called Spearfish, is to all, without a doubt,
    the "Queen" of all the cow towns in the West!

Clara Keszler, Clearfield, South Dakota area homesteader,
and her flock of chickens.

This gal not only has a cellar, but a frame
addition to her soddy. (Nebraska Sandhills)

# GEEZERS

Father Time and Mother Nature
are an unrelenting pair;
they give you constant aches and pains
and take your teeth and hair.
Like waves pounding on a shoreline,
the years erode your mind.
You can't see without your glasses
and they're always hard to find.

You're memory's undependable
as it kicks in and out;
you've now become a geezer,
that's what life is all about.
You socialize with geezers
and play old geezer games,
and you find yourself flirting with
some poor old geezer dames.

"Geez" is Greek for urine stain;
"ers" means your fly's undone;
you're plagued with constipation
or you got the constant runs.
But as your life unravels
and you get that vacant stare,
the one redeeming factor is
you're usually unaware.

*. . . and after questioning him as to just what he meant by "poor old geezer dames" and not getting a straight answer, I wrote the following:*

# POOR OLD GEEZER DAMES

I blame old Mother Nature
    for the shape my body's in;
I must have ticked her off sometime
    and vengeance is her friend.
From my shoulders to my ankles
    there are hail dents everywhere;
my face is full of wrinkles,
    and I have to dye my hair.

I take some medication
    to exist, I must confess;
to put it rather bluntly
    . . . my body is a mess.
My eyesight left me long ago,
    my hearing's going too;
and fellers never look at me
    the way they used to do.

I see these little fillies with
    their jeans down on their hips,
their skimpy little midriff tops
    and rings hooked on their lips;
I'm afraid if I would dress like that,
    you'd think I was insane;
so I stick to "grandma sweatshirts"
    like other geezer dames.

When elastic's left your bladder,
    and "Beano" is your friend;
everythings a-sagging,
    and your backbone starts to bend;
when you flirt with some old geezer,
    but can't recall his name;
you've joined the ranks of women
    who are *"poor old geezer dames!"*

# GOOD OLD DAYS

I wonder who the person is that one time termed the phrase,
"that life begins at fifty, thus begins the good old days."

It's not what it's cracked up to be, I know 'cause I am here;
these "good old days" are not as good as what they might appear.

The first thing that you notice is your body shifting 'round;
what used to point outward is now pointing to the ground.

Your ears and nose grow larger, you no longer have a lap,
and things you once enjoyed the most is now a handicap.

A feller's hair starts falling out; at least what's on his head,
but grows profusely in his ears and out his nose instead.

A woman's hair gets dull and gray, and then it starts to thin,
but starts appearing on her face, especially on the chin.

Your tongue gets twisted saying things, you often stall and fret
trying to remember names you never should forget.

Your grandkid comes for dinner and you greet him at the door,
before you get his right name out you've called him several more.

Probably what is worst of all, and something we all fear,
is when your friends quit speaking up and you can't seem to hear.

Then you lose your eyesight and you're blinder than a bat;
and last to go is memory ...let's see ...um ...where was I at?

# WHILE-YER-AT-IT

The first year I was "honey" until the baby came,
the twenty years that followed he used "mama" for my name.

Now he calls me "granny" and I do my level best
to not let on it bothers me and something I detest.

But the name he often uses, that's just about as bad
is "While-Yer-At-It" and that's the name that really makes me mad.

He never fails to use it when I'm headed out the door
he hollers: "While-Yer-At-It, will you help me with a chore,

like go and feed the bottle calves and turn the water off
and 'While-Yer-At-It' would you check the feed left in the trough?"

I go to town for groceries; before I get out the door,
he hollers: "While-Yer-At-It, stop by the Co-Op store

'cause we need salt and mineral, then stop by at the vet
to see if Dobbin's coggins test results have come in yet."

Now, this old "While-Yer-At-It" is disgusted through and through,
I'm about to turn the tables and call him a name or two.

But first I should advise that he had best call me "Yvonne"
or this old "while-yer-at-it" just might cook a batch of gone.

I'll tell him point blank, I'm not his granny or his mother,
...but then there is a chance I may not answer to another.

I was steaming all about this when I saw on the TV
Dr. Phil with fighting spouses ...then it came to me

that he could call me names much worse, so I best cool down
and "while I'm at it" get the stuff he needs while I'm in town.

*Summers on the farm when I was growing up were busy, busy days. We raised big gardens, much of which we canned, made into jelly, or dried. Then there was threshing time. We children looked forward to that, however, our mother's anticipation wasn't quite the same. Imagine the baking and cooking required to serve approximately twenty-five hungry men two big meals for three or four days. There were no electric stoves, refrigerators or freezers. I learned in later years how much work that really was. My father and brother would be gone for days helping the neighbors with their harvest, and at last the big steam engine pulling the threshing machine came down our road. When it pulled away, our bins were full of fresh smelling wheat and oats and several big straw stacks stood in the field.*

*The word "mattress" was unknown to us in those days. My parents slept in a feather bed (goose down) and the rest had straw ticks. My dad loaded us and the worn, flattened-out ticks into a wagon and out to that new straw pile we went. The old straw was emptied out and the ticks stuffed with new straw. How anxious we were to go to bed that night!*

*by my great aunt, Clara Kayton Larsen (1897 -1981)*

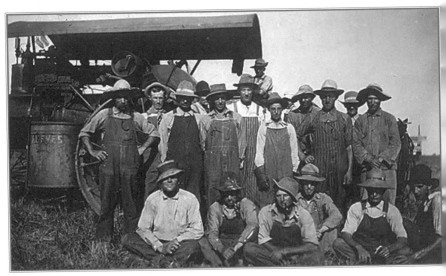

A threshing crew waiting for dinner – Butler County, Nebraska

# THAT OLD FELT HAT

There's a hat rack made of antlers that he'd found out on the range,
  it's on the back porch wall there by the door;
and on it hangs an old felt hat, he hung it there one day,
  and then he never wore it anymore.

She never took it down, although some people thought she should,
  but she says it's more than just a weathered hat;
'cause it holds so many memories of happy days gone by
  so she leaves it hanging right there where it's at.

She recalls when she first saw him, he sure did catch her eye
  and she hoped that he would ask her to the dance.
Weeks later he confessed that he really wanted to
  but he didn't think a cowpoke had a chance.

She remembers when he bought that hat and took it from the box
  and how it fit so perfect on his head;
and the first time that he wore it was a day she won't forget
  'cause it was on the day that they were wed

He wore it just for good for prob'ly twenty years,
  'till his everyday one finally met its end.
From that day on the two of them were never far apart;
  that hat to him was just like an old friend.

She looks at it and thinks about the man she always loved
  . . . the two of them made such a happy pair.
They weathered storms together and had many good times too;
  and now you know just why she leaves it there.

She knows it won't be long 'till she will join him at the throne
  and hopes when she's on heaven's welcome mat,
he'll be waiting just inside, grinning ear-to-ear,
  and she'll see him once again in that old hat.

Mary Bigler, the daughter of a Tripp County homesteader.

## RANCHWIFE IN THE MAKING

Poor Jaydn doesn't know it,
    but was born here to the land;
perhaps that's why she's called on
    when they need another hand.

She doesn't go to school,
    'cause she's only five years old;
but there's no better help
    at driving cattle, so I'm told.

And when they practice roping
    she's the one that runs the gate;
she should not be so willing
    'cause it just might be her fate.

I can just about imagine
    in another year or two,
they'll teach her how to do the chores
    and help to feed a crew.

She's a ranch wife in the making,
    but I guess out here that's life.
She's in training for a future
    as a cattle rancher's wife!

# TRUTH IN ADVERTISING

She was lonely in the city with a life she'd learn to hate
and thought that it would help if she could find herself a mate.

For months she searched the classifieds. . . the "lonely people" kind
and visualized the type of man that she would like to find.

Alas, she happened on an ad that really caught her eye
and knew at once that this would be the perfect kind of guy.

The ad read he was searching for a kind and loving wife,
one who liked to cook and would enjoy his country life.

It said he lived alone on a large Wyoming spread
...her heart began to flutter from the ad that she'd just read.

Romance began to spark as they courted through the mail
as both began to thinking that this match could never fail.

She caught a train to Casper, it's a good thing it was night
'cause vision isn't good in a railway station light.

And you know how you can visualize a body and a face
and when you finally meet 'em you were really way off base?

She had seen them in the movies in all those western scenes
. . . the image of a cowboy had for years been in her dreams,

Why, even cowboy poets like Baxter, Jess, and Pat,
are tall and dark and handsome, but this dude was short and fat!

He had a big potato nose, a red and runny eye,
and the cowboy she had dreamed of was a far cry from this guy.

But, there's a lid for every kettle, there is soup for every pot
'cause a fancy, classy city gal was something she was not.

She weighed at least 400 pounds and half her teeth were gone;
as he looked her up and down he got to thinking "something's wrong!"

But she'd come this far to meet him so he best give her the test,
to see how well she'd like it on his ranch out in the West.

The station agent told me that this pair was quite a sight
with 'em wedged into his pickup heading out into the night.

And as you might imagine, it must have been a thrill
when he told her that his home was waiting 'round that distant hill.

She must'a been surprised when he finally came to stop
before a wooden wagon with a rounded canvas top.

She asked him where the house was and he answered "this is it"
although he was concerned as to whether she would fit.

Now, many days have come and gone. . .they make a happy pair,
although they both were fooled, but neither seems to care.

They learned a darned good lesson, and hope you have learned one too
about the ads you happen on...to check 'em through and through,

Just because a man's a rancher doesn't mean he punches cows;
he might live on a hog ranch and be pigging out some sows.

And every city gal don't always come with *savoir faire*,
she might just be a "country hick" and stuck a-living there.

So be careful of the classifieds, better look before you leap;
you could end up in Wyoming on a ranch a-herding sheep!

*Corn cobs was a good source of heat in our old cook stove. I had picked up all these cobs by myself. I was supposed to get my picture taken (which was a rare occasion because we were so hard up) and was I ever disgusted when my brothers and sister got in the picture with me. That's Myron, David, Esther and Earl. I'm the girl on the right. This was in 1926 when I was 10 years old.*

*Ruth Kayton Hanson of Gordon, Nebraska (my mother)*

*Clara Keszler's old cast iron cook stove in the "trees behind a shed." (Clara was a homesteader in our neighborhood.)*

# THAT OLD HOME COMFORT RANGE

Did Grandma ever tell you about that old cast iron range
    that's out there in the trees behind the shed?
It used to be her cook stove in her kitchen on the ranch;
    I'll bet it baked a million loaves of bread.

She said that Granddad bought it when the two were newlywed
    with money from a Percheron colt he'd sold;
they only had a table and a cot and two old chairs,
    and to them that range was worth its weight in gold.

Her kitchen was a gathering place for relatives and friends,
    'course Grandpa, and neighbors stopping by;
she always had a pot of coffee brewing on that stove
    and was always baking cookies, cakes, or pie.

She'd use an iron handle to remove the burner plate;
    then stir the ashes, add a chunk of wood.
I still can see her cooking on that old "Home Comfort Range,"
    and I'll tell you folks, that food was more than good!

She had to haul her water from a well behind the house,
    and on Saturdays she'd get the washtub down.
She'd heat a bunch of water, everyone would take a bath,
    and later, after chores, we'd go to town.

One Saturday they went to town and heard of R.E.A.,
    and Granddad bought a new electric stove.
He thought that she would like it, and hauled that old one out
    and there it sits a-rusting in the grove.

She didn't use it long before her cooking days were done;
    she never lived to see how things would change.
She died a-wishing she could go back home just one more time
    and cook just one more meal on her old range.

*As was stated in this book's introduction, two things many of the pioneer women had in common were making quilts and writing poetry. The photo above is of my husband's grandmother (Jen McMurtry) in her working clothes. They ranched in the Buffalo Flats area Northeast of Ainsworth, Nebraska. A poem had been printed in the local newspaper, which was written by a lady poking fun at the hats worn by the country gals in the Buffalo Flats area. In retaliation, Jen wrote the poem on the following page.*

# A Buffalo Flats Lady

Your contest now is past and done
and we suppose that you had heaps of fun.
But we think it was a dirty trick
to put us in that limerick.

We would gladly wear a Style Shop hat,
you can bet your last thin dime on that.
But we farmers feel lucky for a place to sleep
and likewise all we want to eat.

Our hats are remodeled, that much is true.
But we don't have money; what else could we do?
And we think it was a hateful caper
to advertise that fact in the county paper.

*Written by Jennie McMurtry (1898-1946)*
*Brown County, Nebraska*

Jen was as pretty as any "city gal." Here is her
wedding photo taken on June 1, 1919.

*I wrote this in response to the matter regarding the finding of a cow infected with BSE in Washington State and the chaos that followed:*

# HOW TO CUT TAXES

Dear President Bush,

There are aliens here by the millions
     . . . illegal, and they're all around;
the Border Patrol is out searching
     but hardly a one's ever found.

The CIA and the Army,
     Marines and the Air Force too,
have been combing the hills of Afghanistan,
     while "Bin" just keeps slipping on through.

There are thousands of folks that are wanted
     by the police and the great  F.B.I.
I think those departments are useless,
     and a big waste of taxes, here's why:

When one Holstein cow met her maker
     at a plant up in Washington State,
in no time they knew where she came from
     and the source of the feed that she'd ate.

They found where her offspring were grazing
     . . . solved all this in less than a day!
They got lots of press and instilled lots of fear
     in a story that won't go away.

So, I think if I was the President
     of this "home of the free and the brave"
I close up all those departments
     and think of the money I'd save.

I'd hire a few veterinarians
      ...a few that would work for short pay;
and call it the *"Mad Cow Militia,*
      *a branch of the U.S.D.A."*

I'd sic this new branch on Bin Laden,
      and give them the run of the Hill;
this could create more excitement
      than when Monica visited Bill!

Just imagine how good you'll be looking
      with the "State of the Nation" this fall;
by closing these other departments,
      you'd have refunds galore for us all.

They'd be carving your face on Mt. Rushmore;
      you'd be leading the list of "who's who;"
All of them Democrats would not have a chance,
      as the nation all rallies 'round you.

With the state of affairs all in order,
      and allies a-wondering "how"
with one explanation you'd tell 'em,
      "it's the result of a single mad cow."

This nation would once again prosper
      with very few taxes to pay,
and we'd credit the *"Mad Cow Militia,*
      *a branch of the USDA!"*

# WHY HIS EARS ARE SWOLLEN

He criticized my cookin'
           didn't care for what I'd bake,
and wished I'd fix him biscuits
           like his mama used to make.

He said I hid his socks,
           his underwear and  ties;
although the place I hid 'em
           was right before his eyes.

I'd hear how mama helped him
           sortin' cattle through the gate;
and even do the chores for him
           when he was runnin' late.

Now, I know I'm far from perfect
           but I try my level best,
and from his constant bickering
           I thought I'd like a rest.

So, last night after hearing
           how he didn't like my stew
I boxed his little ears
           just like his mama used to do!

# WHAT I REALLY NEED'S A WIFE

I've got so danged much stuff to do, I work from sun to sun,
got a great big yard to care for and the housework's needing done.
I was cleaning out the horse barn when I heard my hubby say
that he needed me to help him go and mow a field of hay.

I had to run some cows in, and go fix a gate that's down
then go and get repairs from the tractor shop in town.
There's so much work to do when you live a rancher's life,
that I think what I am needing is to get myself a wife!

I'll bet this South Dakota homesteader would like to find a wife.

*In the spring of 2005, it was reported that test results by a scientific group in Norway found that lobsters did not feel pain when dropped live into boiling water. I found this somewhat amusing (perhaps due to my Norwegian roots) and found myself writing the following poem.*

# THE  LOBSTER  TEST

"It's cruel for a lobster to be dropped into a pot
and see it thrashing  painfully in water boiling hot!"

This cry was heard around the world as PETA made their claim,
while picketing the restaurants and those who are to blame.

Norway got real nervous when the protests hit their shore
fearing soon the PETA folks would start including even more,

like cod and pickled herring, and they knew they'd dare not risk
the thought of PETA picketing their precious lutefisk!

So the parliament in Oslo thought they should perform a test
to prove the PETA folks all wrong and put this thing to rest.

They'd need a volunteer to prove that lobsters feel no pain
when dropped in boiling water, but their search was all in vain;

that is until they called upon their kin in North Dakota,
who helped to get the message out to fill this one-man quota.

The critics said that no one would be dumb enough to dive
into the boiling water, 'cause there's no way they'd survive.

When alas!   They found a gunsel by the name of Ole Svensen
who said that threatening Lutefisk had sure got his attention!*

*"Ya shure, ya got a volunteer, I'll yump dare in da vat!
And if it hurts I'll yeller out and tell ya folks 'bout dat!"*

So right up there in Bismarck on a cold and frosty morn,
the test would be completed and a hero would be born.

A giant vat was filled with water from the nearby river
and a fire built beneath it, as the folks began to quiver.

But Ole never faltered and the time would soon arrive
when North Dakota's volunteer would make his famous dive.

The "Sons of Norway" gathered round, when Ole plugged his nose
and bravely jumped into the vat wearing nothing but his clothes.

If a dunk in boiling water would cause pain, there's no doubt,
that the world would know the outcome if they heard poor Ole shout.

And while the folks were waiting, not a word from Ole came
so they called the test successful, backing Norway's claim to fame.

Although no one has heard or seen poor Ole since that day
there's a sense of satisfaction that the protests went away.

To honor him the restaurants are serving a new dish
and folks are lining up to eat this special kind of fish.

Instead of cooking lobster like the way that we all know,
they're dropping them into a vat of boiling Oleo.


*ya shure, ya betcha, attention does rhyme with Svensen if you
pronounce it like a Norvegian does . . . ie: attenshen

On September 1, 1909, Carl Keszler and his new bride left Lancaster County, Nebraska, in a covered wagon, driving Jack and Jenny, their fine span of mules. Behind the loaded wagon was their horse and "spooning" buggy filled with dishes and provisions. It took two weeks to make the trip to Dallas and from there they would go on to their claim in Tripp County, South Dakota, which was three miles North and four miles West of Clearfield.

While in Dallas a man offered them $1800 for their claim. Carl asked his wife, Clara, if he should take it. Her reply was that after coming this far she was going on out to see the claim. That very night they camped out three miles South of McNeely and the coyotes howled all night. He asked, "Well, what do you think now?" Her reply was, "I will have to learn to use the rifle."

*from the memoirs of Carl Keszler, deceased*

Some neighbors visiting Carl and Clara Keszler (Carl is sitting on the right corner of wagon and Clara is standing). In front are their two mules, Jack and Jenny.

# DINING OUT

When you live out in the country, it's really quite a treat
when, maybe once or twice a year, you might go out to eat.

It happened once last summer after helping put up hay,
my husband asked me if I would like to eat in town that day.

Well, I was quick to answer "Yes," then hurried to prepare;
I bathed and changed to better clothes and fixed my windblown hair.

In nothing flat, our pickup truck was headed down the lane;
a dinner date with hubby was like lighting an old flame!

I'm visualizing candlelight as music softly plays.
imagining the kindly things that he would probably say!

And as the pickup bounced along, I dreamed of even more;
when soon we pulled into the town up to the old feed store.

I told him I would wait outside while he picked up some feed;
as the guy that usually waits on him don't have a lot of speed.

Besides my shoes were killing me, I thought I'd rest my feet.
He said: "You'd better come on in, if you would like to eat."

He pointed to a banner on the door that I could read,
for the annual pancake supper at the local Feed and Seed!

*In July of 2004, the Academy of Western Artists held a team writing competition during their annual convention. There was a division for song writing as well as poetry, and both were required to have the theme, "Only a Cowboy Knows." Pat Richardson and I entered the poetry writing competition, however, I was just recovering from surgery removing a brain tumor, so Pat had to write most of this poem as well as perform it. Fortunately for me we won first place! Pat also won the song writing competition with Kip Calahan. Here is our poem:*

## BENNY'S FUNERAL
### *(co-written with Pat Richardson)*

A bone of contention from Fargo to Dallas
    pertains to the wisdom that cowboys possess.
No two agree what a cowboy should know,
    it depends on which region you hail from, I guess.

Ben was my guru, my mentor, my hero;
    he practically raised me since I was a teen.
Taught me to ride and rope with the best of them,
    here's Benny's story, you'll see what I mean:

Ben was a cowboy, lived south of Sonoma,
    he lived with no visible means of support.
He taught us what only a cowboy would know,
    then, nearing' ninety, his life was cut short.

Benny bucked off of his favorite cow horse,
    the buck-off was fatal he didn't survive.
We loaded him up in the mortician's outfit
    with the services held at Ben's favorite dive.

They couldn't embalm him, 'cause he was too pickled,
    but they dressed him up in his favorite old suit.
He looked mighty lifelike, laid out in his coffin,
    an' folks paid respects to the ornery ol' coot.

We hired some strippers to work Benny's funeral
   in hopes of attracting a sizeable mob;
the preacher, distracted, made several lewd comments
   an' excused it by sayin', "Just doin' my job."

Nobody wanted to act as a pallbearer,
   "too bulky, too heavy, an' too hot," they whined.
His widow, though crippled, gave 'em all a good cussing
   using such language the bar had her fined.

She rode in the hearse, up front with the driver,
   an' played with the levers, the buttons, an' knobs;
the back doors opened, an' out dumped ol' Benny
   the minute she pulled the wrong thing-a-muh-bob.

The strippers were strippin', the mourners were mournin'
   an' nobody noticed ol' Ben had fell out;
several cars hit him in rapid succession,
   his "corpus delicti" was battered about.

We got him re-loaded, (at least the big pieces)
   an' soon got things rollin' an' lined out again.
The parts we missed made stains on the roadway
   an' the city paved over the rest of ol' Ben.

So here's to ol' Benny, a cowboy'n legend;
   he taught us all what a cowboy should know.
Even in death ol' Ben was flamboyant;
   he "cadavered-up", an' went on with the show.

*One of the nicest things about the Western Entertainment business is the many wonderful people you meet and become friends with. One such friend is the great Texas singer, Jean Prescott. Jean has made several songs out of my poems, however, the following poem was written by the two of us, then made into a song.*

# MONEY TALKS
*(co-written with Jean Prescott)*

He was born right there in Texas
    though he was darned-sure "Scotch,"
each time he'd tighten up his belt
    he'd take another notch.
After years of pinchin' pennies
    with a close eye on the cash
they paid off land and cattle
    and built up quite a stash.

He took the money they had saved
    and stuffed it in a sack
...hid it 'neath the floorboards
    in a corner of their shack.
Later in his golden years,
    to pass the time away,
he'd get that sack of money
    and count it every day.

Then every time he counted it
    he'd beg her to comply,
that she would take that bag of cash
    on the day he'd die
and put it in his casket
    and leave it there with him
so if he got to heaven
    it would help to get him in.

I saw her at the funeral
    ...she was looking debonair;
I asked her if that sack of cash
    was resting with him there.
She said she thought of his new home
    thinking she would like one too,
so bought one with the money
    and gave him an I.O.U.

CHORUS:   She said, "You can't take it with you
                when your days on earth are through.
                The Lord don't want your money
                ...all he wants is you!

*My poetry writing friend, Pat Richardson, and I were asked to write a poem for an upcoming book written by Billie Thornburg about the brothels in North Platte, Nebraska. This is our poem:*

## CASTING STONES
*(co-written with Pat Richardson)*

Some women turn their noses up and would not dare to greet
this lady of the evening when they meet her on the street;

and when a feller meets her, he is quick to turn his head
for fear she'll recognize him, which is something he would dread.

Don't be quick at passing judgment 'till you've walked where she has trod;
though you may not want to hear this . . . you both were made by God.

And we do not know what prompted her to enter this profession,
but who of us is sinless when we make a true confession?

Did she become a harlot out of want, or 'cause of need?
Perhaps she had some loved ones that she felt compelled to feed.

It's possible she started out a believer still, in love,
when some circumstances changed her into a soiled dove.

How she makes a living may to you seem like a crime,
but it's an old profession that's withstood the test of time;

But when there's troubled waters, or rough ways on your route
it's the one you treated badly that's the first to help you out.

So in essence what I'm saying, maybe take a closer look,
'cause it's hard to read the pages through the cover of a book.

Nebraska Sandhiller, Billie Snyder (circa 1925) showing off a good day's hunt. Note the large pile of cow chips also known as "prairie fuel."

Above is Billie's brother, Miles, with a coyote he had, in front of the winter supply of cow chips.

# THE ORIGIN OF MOUNTAIN OYSTERS

Mankind has had its mysteries and probably always will
like how they walked four miles to school and both ways were uphill;

or about the chicken and the egg . . . just which was the first one?
Or when you're doing nothing how d'ya know when you are done?

But the thing that really baffles me, and 'bout drives me insane,
is who discovered "mountain oysters" and who gave them that name?

It's a rather fishy title . . . they don't come from the sea,
and they don't resemble mountains 'cause they are little as can be.

Folks call the other cattle parts, like liver, tongue or brain
exactly what they represent with no need to explain.

There's something really curious about this form of meat,
just who discovered those darned things as something good to eat?

Perhaps it was a woman who had vengeance on her mind
because of some dang feller who had treated her unkind.

Did she fix 'em as a warning that she too could play the game
when she found out that his working late was with some other dame?

Did she see them working cattle and fetch 'em from the smoke,
then throw some in the frying pan and serve them as a joke?

I hope that modern science with the help of DNA
can solve this age-old question and can put this thing away.

Until they do I'll wonder who the person is to blame
who gave those bovine testicles that "mountain oyster" name!

# CUTTIN' KATIE

She had come in from the country for supplies, and stopped to eat;
  when a city slicker spied her and he slid right in the seat.
He said that he was lonely and he hoped she'd let him stay;
  he would gladly buy her dinner . . . it sure would make his day.

He flirted with this lady who had come in from a ranch,
  and asked a stupid question that soon killed his only chance.
As they both looked at the menu, he must'a thought her dumb,
  'cause he asked her if she knew where mountain oysters come from?

She looked at him with scorn, made him shift there in his seat,
  saying she had gathered more of them than he could ever eat.
And then went into detail how the harvesting was done.
  Of all the jobs she had to do, she thought this one was fun!

She told him she had castrated many calves and goats;
  dogs, and cats, and chickens, and a hog barn full of shoats.
She said she'd pro'bly cut at least a thousand head of sheep
  and she fixed a cheat'n husband once when he was sound asleep!

She pulled a knife out of her purse, in a rather subtle way,
  saying she would show him how it's done if he had time to stay.
They say the color left him as he leaped upon his feet
  leaving skid marks on the carpet as he made a fast retreat!

Katie ate alone, although he left her with the tab;
  and she later told her husband 'bout the lie she told that lad
that is holed up in his townhouse with a mind that's full of scars,
  and will never go near women found in restaurants or bars.

They call her "Cuttin' Katie" though she doesn't have a clue
  how the castration's done . . . it's something she don't do.
But the moral of the story is to help protect your wife,
  make sure that she knows how to lie, and always packs a knife!

# WATCH WHAT YOU PRAY FOR

I believe in God above and know he answers prayers.
I'll bet he knows it's dry down here and of course, our Savior cares.

Don't think that He's forgot us, and He's not trying to be mean
just 'cause it never seems to rain; He's testing us, it seems.

Remember Ninety-seven and the winter that we had?
We hadn't had no weather in a coon's age near that bad!

The feed and tanks and fences were all buried deep in snow;
and temperatures for many days stayed 'round 15 below.

Well, I prayed that it would warm up, and sure enough, it did.
That summer it got hotter than a boiling kettle lid!

But shoot, we got good rainfall and the grass was lush and green;
the dams were running over, as were creeks and ponds and streams.

But apparently some farmer couldn't plant his crops in time;
you know when things aren't perfect how they always seem to whine.

I can just about imagine that he went to God in prayer
and asked if He would help him get his crops put in out there.

Now, please don't find me critical, or one to be complaining,
but I'd like to find that so-and-so who prayed that it'd quit raining!

# FEED SALESMEN DON'T LIE

We were sure struggling a-raisin' them cattle,
it seemed that a profit was not to be found;
Our debt was a-growing and we were sure worried
until a feed salesman stopped by on his round.

He showed us a product that he was a-selling
that was guaran-damn-teed to add fifty pounds;
only a fool would fail to not buy it
we knew at that moment salvation was found.

It's normal to wean off a five hundred pounder;
a few good bull calves might weigh a tad more.
But buying that feed would sure be the ticket
for adding more pounds, then our profits would soar.

That got us to thinking about all the products
that promise to increase your profits and gain.
We bought us some Smartlic, some fly tags and Warbex,
and soy-based high protein energized grain.

Pfizer invented some weight-gain injections,
we bought Ivomec to rid parasites.
Lick tubs were added to our cattle rations
with special injections to whet appetites.

Then a computer with cattle gain programs
was something we thought would be handy to have;
and we were astonished when checking the outcome
that we would be weaning some thousand pound calves!

We bought a new pickup, a trailer, a tractor,
with no money down 'till we sell in the fall;
The profits we get from the use of these products
should pay off our debt plus cover this all.

So if you are planning to make it in ranching
you'd best follow suit or your business will die,
and if you would like, I'll send by that salesman
'cause we are aware that feed salesmen don't lie!

Fannie & Henry Hookstra, Butler County, Nebraska,
checking on some hogs in the shed. (my great aunt and uncle)

Yes, even ranchers had hogs as is evidenced by this photo of the
Read Ranch, a pioneer ranch in Tripp County, South Dakota.

# THE WAITRESS

We were broke when he said "Honey, we sure could use some money
    do you think that you could get a job in town?"
Well I was sick of cookin' but I thought I'd best go lookin'
    and it wasn't long until I nailed one down.

The best one in my job hunt was in the local rest'rant
    but it was not the job of slinging hash;
No, it was waitin' tables where I thought that I'd be able
    to make good tips and earn some extra cash.

I was good at table waitin' but there's one thing I was hate'n
    it was when those blasted coffee drinkers came;
every morning just at ten, at least a dozen would come in
    and they would nearly drive us all insane.

After they would gather, they'd start talkin' 'bout the weather,
    as for gossip, they could really dig up some;
they would hit on what was new (though they might not have a clue)
    and could solve most everything in Washington.

Then you'd hear about the gout, how a cataract came out;
    while one relived a recent colon scope.
Their prostrates were discussed while they called for second cups,
    (it's no wonder that the poor darned things were broke!)

I cancelled news subscriptions; don't ever get prescriptions,
    and the doctor bills I've saved is really nice.
Everything I need to know I get from listen'n to them blow,
    from the markets to sound medical advice.

Well, now we're sittin' fine, got our finances in line
    since I started workin' at that eatin' shack;
and it ain't from my slavin', but from money I been savin'
    just a-listenin' to those coffee drinkers yak!

*This poem was written in answer to a poem entitled "The Bra" which was written by Bill Hirschi of Rexburg, Idaho, and perhaps the most plagiarized poem in existence. All of the female entertainers in the Cowboy Gathering Circuit were tired of hearing it, so I wrote this in retaliation:*

# THE TRUTH ABOUT:
## THE BRA

I was working in the dress shop when a dude came in that day
    and we were quite amused at him, that's one thing I will say.
It was about the strangest thing I think we'd ever saw
    when he told us he had come in there to buy his wife a bra.

Now, I have heard some windies and been told a lot of lies;
    after all, I raised teenagers, and dated cheating guys.
He wasn't buying no brassiere to take home to his wife;
    it's obvious he's one of those who lives a double life.

I doubt he even has a wife, if he would just fess up,
    or she must be quite a looker if she wears that big 'a-cup!
And did you ever hear of women ever asking guys
    to go to town and buy a bra and not give him a size?

I wasn't born just yesterday...I've been around the block;
    and I can spot a liar when he first begins to talk.
He might look like a cowboy as he dishes out that line,
    but a sales clerk in a dress shop can spot one every time.

Some are wanting dresses and some want underwear,
    and always say "it's for my wife," but we are all aware
that these items they are buying are really for themselves
    as they eyeball lacy garments on the racks and on the shelves.

And when you ask for sizes you can always bet those guys
    will answer quick: "I do not know, but she's about my size."
But to come into a dress shop to buy a bra? My word!
    And use a hat for cup size is the dumbest thing I've heard!

This poor horse must be wondering what that contraption is!

But yes, indeed, the automobile was soon to be a "must have"
item in the country as well as the city.

# MY DRIVER

There's not much he can do now
     since he had that mini-stroke;
and the medicine they've got him on
     has darned near got us broke.

Both his eyes have cataracts,
     he needs some hearing aids;
can't see or hear, but worse than that
     his memory often fades.

He used to do a lot of work,
     but now it's quite a chore
to just get up and dress himself
     and shuttle 'cross the floor.

But one thing I am thankful for
     sides the fact he's still alive,
is when I want to go somewhere
     I still have him to drive!

*As we all know, farmers have a habit of complaining, especially when it's dry, which is most of the time it seems. This farmer had a problem.*

# A FARMER'S WORST NIGHTMARE

A terrible dilemma
was a-facing Farmer Brown,
he was getting daily rains
that was soaking up the ground.

His seed had gone unplanted
and it was about too late
to get his corn crop listed;
it was about to be his fate.

There's nothing worse for farmers
than to not plant crops on time,
and when things don't go perfect,
you know they like to whine.

Well, the rainfall just had ended
the driest spell in years,
and another year like that
would be the worst of fears.

Because of last year's drought,
he had to welcome all the rain;
and the worst of all of this
was that he did not dare complain!

*This poem was written on September 3, 2005, one week after Hurricane Katrina hit the Louisiana Gulf Coast area, causing widespread disaster in that area, including the dike failure that virtually destroyed the city of New Orleans.*

# REALITY CHECK

It's just a normal thing I guess, when living in the West,
to complain about the life out here when things are not the best.

We gripe about the cost of goods, the lack of rain and such;
how taxes just keep going up and fuel costs too much.

Then grumble 'bout the weather, from the heat, to ice and snow,
and how it's hard to feed the stock at twenty-some below.

The last few days were different. I've heard no one complain
'bout the cost of goods or taxes, or how bad we're needing rain.

I'm like the other folks around, with thoughts of New Orleans,
and the tragedy that hit there . . . the devastating scenes.

I hope those poor folks realize how much the nation cares,
and how they're heavy on our minds . . . the subject of our prayers.

We once again reflect on just how fragile life can be
with many lives affected by one single tragedy.

From the time that you are born until they load you in the hearse,
we're reminded that when things go wrong, they always could be worse.

I reflect upon my life and find my future's not so dim
'cause their cups are nearly empty and mine's filled up to the brim.

*In the spring of 1889 I moved into South Dakota and located on the Bad River, 22 miles West of Ft. Pierre. This land had previously been on an Indian reservation and had been thrown open for settlement. I started a little store and asked that a postoffice be established. My request was granted and the name Bovine given to the postoffice. The postoffice has given place to Capa of the present day.*

*Ben Arnold (1844 -1922) from his biography,*
*"The Exploits of Ben Arnold"*

*\*Ben Arnold was my great grandfather. It was while running the post office at Bovine (now Capa), that my grandmother was born in 1891.*

# A GOOD NAME

There's a place over East in a valley
      where the buildings are weathered and old;
it once was somebody's homestead
      full of dreams of a future, I'm told.

I wonder each time I go by there
      just how long they have been all alone;
how long that it's been since that house there
      was once some family's home.

The barn is still standing quite stately,
      though the roof has begun caving in;
and I'm sure that it won't be too long now
      'fore it's downed by a strong prairie wind.

It's so sad to see just the remnants
      of what once was somebody's pride.
Did they leave because of some hard times
      or was it because someone died?

You can see where they planted some lilacs,
      there's a piece of an old iron fence;
a rusty old pump still sits on a well,
      though I doubt it's been used ever since.

I guess it is like many other
      old places that's left to decay,
reminding us time waits for no one,
      and that too soon there will come a day

when our lives will be like that homestead;
      and treasures that we might possess
will weather and long be forgotten,
      no matter how great your success.

The only thing folks will remember
      are things that you do and you say;
the kindness you show to a neighbor
      or a stranger you pass on the way.

It don't matter how many possessions
      you've gathered in life to lay claim,
the one thing that won't be forgotten
      is the fact that you had a good name.

# THE VETERINARIAN'S GOAT

Our vet, he had a little goat that was always in the way;
he'd put it in its special pen but it would never stay.

He thought perhaps if it got bred that she might settle down,
and had heard about a Billy Goat standing stud just South of town.

He called upon the owner of this goat world's finest sire,
who said, "Just bring your nanny out, we'll see what might transpire."

He had some trouble loading her, it took an hour or two.
You know how stubborn females are when it comes to pleasing you.

The rancher helped unload the goat and put her in a shed
where she would spend the next few days, at least until she's bred.

The vet paid the deposit, then headed back to town.
The next day he received a call that was sure to bring a frown.

You see, the rancher called the vet and put him in a tether
because the goat he'd brought to breed turned out to be a wether.

The vet picked up his wether, and made one last request,
to please not let this story out.  It was too late . . . you guessed.

So now you know the story and I sure don't mean to gloat,
but it's true about a rancher who got a veterinarian's goat!

# DUCT TAPE

There's a simple little product that is known, without a doubt
      as the number one invention of all time.
It's in every glove compartment, in every saddle bag,
      and is even used by cops for fighting crime.

It is used for mending everything from clothes to plastic seats,
      and holes in screens those blasted crickets ate;
it's a miracle for everyone that's ever lived or walked,
      the handy silver product called "Duct Tape."

It has helped the most unhandy man to fix most anything
      from eyeglass frames to plugging leaky tanks,
you can patch a broken window, or a radiator hose;
      to the guy that thought it up, we all give thanks!

Loose tile in the bathroom, or a worn-out tablecloth,
      just two more things this handy tape can mend.
It'll stop the feathers leaking out of your old down-filled coat,
      and is used to wrap a present for a friend.

You can use it for a band-aid, to remove a stubborn wart,
      and it's used to wrap around a saddle horn;
it's been used to fix a handle on a hammer or a hoe,
      and hold the soles on boots that's old and worn.

It's the greatest thing since baling wire to use around the house
      on things like stool lids and cupboard doors;
one guy used so much duct tape fixing things around the home
      that his wife thought it was part of her décor.

But just when he was thinking that it never could be beat,
      that Duct Tape was just something to beheld,
I heard him holler: "Mama, you had better come here quick!
      I found us something new, called J.B. Weld!"

# I DUNNO

There's a naughty little poltergeist that lives here in my house
  but the only one that knows him seems to be my loving spouse.
The kids, they used to know him but they've grown and moved away
  and I wish he'd moved along with them . . . instead he chose to stay.

He has a name, it's "I Dunno" and as welcome as a mouse
  'cause he's the one that seems to do the bad things 'round the house.
I'd find food on the carpet, or I'd come home to a mess,
  then ask who was responsible, but no one would confess

except a kid, or hubby, when I'd ask 'em one more time.
  The answer would be "I Dunno" who tracked in dirt and grime.
"I Dunno" has broken dishes and has tore a lot of clothes
  and accidentally ran the mower over garden hose.

The next time hubby hollers that he needs some help outside,
  or wonders where some tools are he thinks I always hide;
or needs to move some cattle and wonders, "would I go?"
  I'll just suggest he asks his little buddy, "I Dunno."

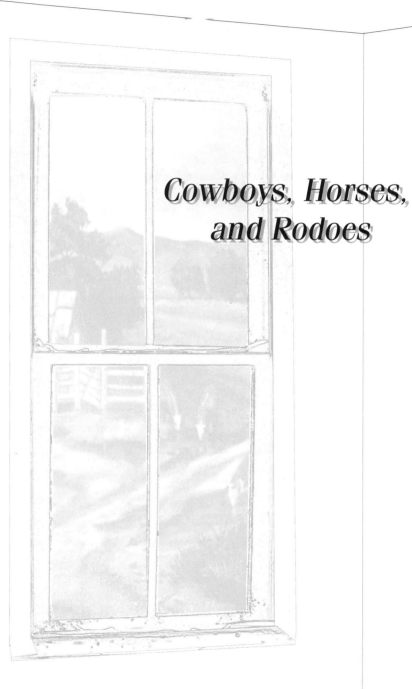

# Cowboys, Horses,
# and Rodoes

# OLD FOLKS RODEO

There's a great association where old cowboys go and play;
　　it's like a big reunion for the hands of yesterday.
It started out "Old Timers," now they call it "Senior Pro."
　　Whatever one might call it, it's an "Old Folks Rodeo."

Old Cowboys still like whiskey or a can or two of beer,
　　but usually bring a grandkid 'long to help 'em drive and hear.
They often drive big motor homes, the latest of its kind
　　with fancy matching trailers to pull along behind.

Their gear bags look like drugstores, full of analgesic balm,
　　magnets and Viagra, and some pills to keep 'em calm.
The "chicks" that used to hang around in 1962
　　are now "old hens" still hanging 'round, and sometimes in a stew.

I thought I'd like to take one in and see how they are run
　　and learned that Old Folks Rodeos are sure a lot of fun.
It started with the crowning of this year's Senior Queen;
　　I don't know the criteria, but it was quite a scene.

The one they crowned had won the banner fair and square, of course,
　　but when she went to run her lap she couldn't mount her horse.
Thank goodness for a gate man who helped her brace her feet,
　　while her predecessor pushed and pulled and got her in the seat.

The entries in the barebacks are usually slim to none,
　　but broncs and bulls are better, though they seldom cover one.
They usually have some pickup men as green as they can be,
　　but, what-the-heck, they usually never work too hard, you see.

Then comes the tie-down roping (that's what they call it now);
　　a friend of ours was entered and he caught his calf somehow.
He lumbered down and flanked that calf...one hand went underneath
　　he yanked that string out of his mouth, but dang! There went his teeth!

They found 'em when the raked the ground at barrel racing time;
　　those teeth were awful dirty, they were caked with dirt and grime.
And speaking of the barrels, there is no where you could find
　　any better horses, and this is not a state of mind.

But the horses run the pattern better than their riders do,
    like when 'Ol Dobbin left that gal back there at barrel two!
Another failed to make the turn at barrel number one,
    but gravity has shifted since the days when they were young.

Thank God they left team roping for the last event that night;
    I'll bet there were two hundred teams and it was quite a sight.
It's evident that this event is sweeping 'cross the land,
    but good old cowboys never roped with "golf gloves" on their hand.

The old cowboy's short on manners and he says just what he feels
    when his arthritic partner ups and misses both the heels.
One header really nailed one, but it was hard to cope,
    when his partner got excited and dropped the doggone rope!

I'm sure you've heard it said that every dog should have its day;
    and only right that old cowboys should have a chance to play.
So, if you crave excitement and you wonder where to go,
    may I suggest you go to see an "Old Folks Rodeo."

Vintage photo of champion bronc rider Clifford Lyons on Cricket
at the White River, South Dakota Frontier Days Rodeo

*This is about my husband's good rope horse "Punch."*

# A HORSE NOBODY'D WANT

I bought "Punch" from a trader who didn't know his age;
and said he'd lost the papers but "he's ten" by what he'd gauge.
T'was a darned good looking gelding, but looks are just skin-deep;
it's heart and disposition that wins money you can keep.

At first he'd hump and try to buck, but that was not as bad
as when you'd go to bridle him...the worst I ever had.
He'd obviously been beaten on the head and by the ears;
you still can't touch his right one and it's now been several years.

After weeks of gentle treatment, that horse became my friend,
he paid me back ten-fold the way things turned out in the end.
And why someone was mean to him, I often wonder why,
but know there are bad horsemen...a fact we can't deny.

I trained him for a calf horse and a good one he become;
he'd track a calf, stop real good, and my, how he could run!
We tried to sell him several times but no one wanted him,
they'd take him home and try him out and bring him back again.

One old dolly thought he'd make a good horse for her son,
but tried him out and changed her mind before the deal was done.
Some windy guy from Texas saw him workin' rope one day
and offered cold hard cash if he could have a year to pay.

There were several tough young ropers that turned their back on him
and searched for better horses that just might help 'em win.
Then my buddy, Arlen, told me not to sell that horse
'cause he might be a winner, and he was right, of course.

Soon the horse nobody'd wanted started turning lots of heads
'cause together we were winning as the word began to spread
that this was quite a rope horse, then calls began to come
to see if I would sell this horse they'd heard was number one.

I'd say, "this horse is not for sale" and that just suits me fine
'cause he and I are having fun a-winnin' most the time.
And when I want another horse to rope on, I will try
to find myself another one that no one wants to buy.

My husband Glen Hollenbeck winning a round on "Punch" at a US Calf
Roping held at Johnstown, Nebraska, in the summer of 2003. Glen and
the horse won the US Calf Roping Finals that fall, bringing home a sack
full of money, a buckle, a championship horse trailer and other prizes.

Larry Hollenbeck hazing steer on Red (Glen Hollenbeck dogging)

Our son, Shawn Hollenbeck , tying goats off of
Red at the South Dakota State 4H Finals

*This is a poem about perhaps the best horse that ever lived on our ranch.*

# PUTTING DOWN OLD RED

It's been said that every cowboy, if he's lucky in his life,
has one good dog, one good horse, and of course, has one good wife.

To give one up is something he'd avoid if he could
'cause parting is a sorrow. . . if parting is for good.

Without a doubt his best one, a horse he called "Old Red"
was running out of sunsets, which is something we all dread.

But Father Time is brutal and he treats us all the same;
he paid Old Red a visit and he left him old and lame.

And the winters in Dakota can kill the young and strong
'though we kept him close and nursed him, we knew it wasn't long

'till the weather and his lameness would slowly spell the end,
and no one ever wants that type of death for an old friend.

I knew that it was up to me, and what I'd have to do
'cause it's hard to put a horse down after all that they'd been through.

One day when he went riding and would not be home 'till night
I called a vet to help me out, and knew it'd be all right;

after all, I wasn't so attached 'cause Red was not my mount
and the times that I had rode him were just too few to count.

But by the time the vet arrived, I had time to reflect
about the many rodeos and money we'd collect

from all those tie-down ropings that Old Red had helped him win,
from mounting other ropers, and from picking up on him.

Then I thought about our little kids, when they were starting out,
how that old horse had taught them what "first place" was all about.

Our trophy case is full of plaques and ribbons that they won
in goats and poles and barrels, and my that horse could run!

I went and got a halter and a bucket full of oats
and dear Old Red came up to me and nuzzled on my coat

just like so many times before, but this time was the end;
the vet was here and it was time to put down our old friend.

I found out just how tough I was; I guess I must'a lied
when I told myself, "it won't be bad" ...the bad part's how I cried.

I could have filled a bucket with all the tears I shed,
and I hope you never face a task like putting down Old Red.

My husband, Glen, roping on Red

Our daughter, Teresa, pole bending on Old Red
at South Dakota State 4H Finals.

*This was a poem I wrote for a poster poem session held at the Arizona Cowboy Poetry Gathering at Prescott in 2005.*

# WHAT A RIDE!

I'm sitting here just thinking
    and wishing I could go
back to the days when I was young
    and worked the rodeo.

Oh, how I used to rope and ride
    . . . they claim I was the best;
but the sun that shone upon me then
    is now setting in the West.

My trophies and my saddles
    are all in the Hall of Fame;
and if you check the record books,
    you still can find my name.

But one award I'll cherish most,
    until my dying day,
is all the many friendships
    that I gathered 'long the way.

There are bumps in life's arena,
    but however rough the ride,
you'll always make the whistle
    with a friend there by your side.

They'll help you top the roughest mounts,
    always pitch you slack;
or grab your cinch and pull it tight,
    then slap you on the back.

So, as I ride into the sunset,
    before I cross that great divide;
I'll tip my hat to all my friends
    and holler: "What a Ride!"

# DON'T EVER JUDGE

You should never judge a cowboy
by the color of his hat;
all good ones don't wear white ones
while just bad ones wear the black.

And you sure can't judge a cowboy
by the clothes he wears, of course,
about the only way to score him
is to see him ride a horse.

It's just like judging people,
and we've done it once or twice;
we've thought someone would be real bad
and find out that they're nice.

You should never judge a person
by the color of their skin;
you just might get to know them
and they'll end up your best friend!

# THE PETA REPORTER

He lay there in a coma
        with stuff dripping in his vein
when she broke into his room
        like she was half-insane.
She only had one question,
        at least that's what she said,
for the cowboy there in traction
        with the bandage on his head.

His jaw was wired shut,
        with a tube so he won't choke,
his arms were solid stitches,
        and most his ribs were broke.
The nurse asked her to leave
        and she didn't want no fights
'cause the priest had just arrived
        to administer Last Rites.

But the lady got real snooty
        and said she must proceed
to get answers she was wanting,
        and never paid no heed,
'cause she had come to question
        that feller on that bed
and she was unconcerned
        that he was close to being dead.

The nurse called in security
        ...they took the lady out,
but as she left the building,
        the folks all heard her shout.
She said "I'm here with PETA
        and I'm gonna file a claim
'cause we feel that cowboy in there
        didn't treat that bull humane!"

# THE OLD COWBOY

I was looking around in a big shopping mall,
   when sitting alone on a bench in the hall
was a weathered old man in a cowboy hat;
   he looked kinda strange in a big place like that.

I walked up to him and I said, "I suppose
   you're an ol' cowhand by the looks of your clothes."
*"Ya guesses me right and a good one,"* he said
   (and the smell of his breath just about knocked me dead!)

*"An' we was lots better than these modern kids,*
   *why, I used to run with a feller named Tibbs;*
*. . .can't remember his name, but at least anyways*
   *they had tougher stock than those kids ride nowadays.*

He went on a-tellin' me 'bout years ago
   when he used to win all of the big rodeos.
He rattled off names of some horses he'd rode
   and according to him, he'd never been throwed.

He claimed they dogged steers that weighed half a-ton
   and roping back then had to be lots more fun,
'cause the calves that they roped was sure bigger than now
   . . . according to him, 'bout the size of a cow.

In a voice growing louder, and a face turning red:
   *"who'd ever think cowboys'd wear caps on their head?*
*a necklace? or earring? Why, they look a-fright!*
   *. . . wear 'em in my day, you'd ask for a fight!*

*The shirts look like billboards all covered with signs;*
   *you wouldn't be caught in one back in my time.*
*I'll tell you right now, we were tough and were good*
   *an' we acted and dressed like a real cowboy should.*

I was starting to wish that I continued to walk
   'cause the longer I listened, the louder he'd talk.
I quick changed the subject, asked where he called home,
   he said, *"on a ranch, but I don't live alone*

71

*'cause I share my quarters with my youngest grandson,*
  *he's one of these cowboys who don't have no fun.*
*I call him a  modern-day young buckaroo,*
  *he  never drinks whiskey, don't smoke and don't chew.*

As he was a-talking, he rolled up a smoke,
  then lit it an' coughed 'till I thought he would croak.
That brought up something he rolled on his tongue,
  then spit out what looked like a piece of his lung.

Then here came a well-dressed and handsome young guy
  who looked at the smoke as he let out a sigh,
and scolded the man for not quitting for good:
  *"I know that it's hard, but I sure wish you would."*

He told me his name and then shook my hand,
  and said: *"He's my grandpa, and quite an old man.*
*I sure want to thank you for listening to him,*
  *I'm sure 'bout the old days,"* then gave me a grin.

He helped the man up and said:  *"We should go*
  *'cause I have to leave for my next rodeo."*
I couldn't help notice the buckle he wore
  . . .a gold NFR one; must I say more?

Now folks, we've all heard it in so many ways
  how things were much better back in the old days.
I guess the old stories are like a fine wine,
  they keep getting better with the passing of time.

But one thing I learned from the old man that day
  was how fast things change, and how time slips away.
And one thing for sure, we know that it's true
  . . . things aren't as good as what we used to do!

Some Cowboys getting ready for a round up on the
Bert Snyder (Pinnacle Jake) Ranch near Arthur, Nebraska

Cowboys are unsaddled and in the line camp shack on the Bert Snyder Ranch

# NATURE'S CHURCH

Did you ever see the mountains that are covered up with snow,
or watch a setting sun and see its purple afterglow?

Have you ever seen a newborn calf a-wobbling to its feet,
and though it's only minutes old it knows just where to eat?

You can't climb upon a saddle horse and cross the prairie sod,
or see an eagle on the wing and not believe in God.

A cowboy doesn't worship in a building made of stone,
but worships with his Maker out with nature all alone.

His church is in the great outdoors; the valley, heaven's gate,
his favorite hymn's a coyote that is calling to its mate.

And he never does his tithing dropping money in a hand,
it's by being a good caretaker of the creatures and the land

He makes his own communion while a choir of songbirds sing,
. . . cups his hands and drinks the fresh cold water from a spring.

With the budding of the springtime and with autumn's goldenrod
there's no better place to worship than to be out there with God.

So, when you hear a meadowlark that's singing from his perch,
he's inviting you to worship with him there at Nature's Church.

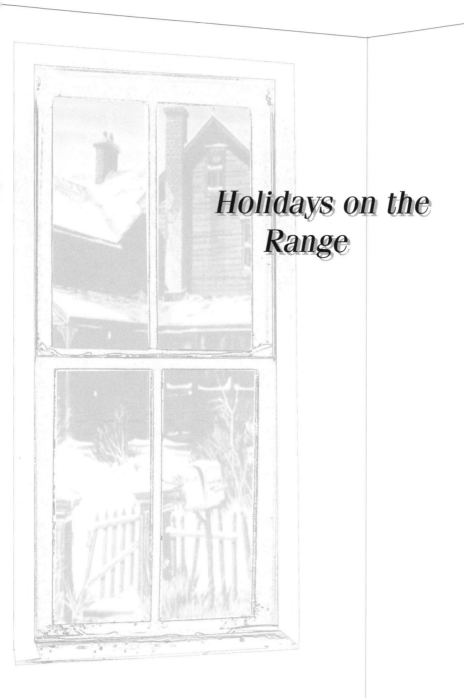

*Holidays on the Range*

# VIRGINIA, I BELIEVE...

Yes, Virginia, I believe there is a Santa Claus;
but I don't think he is a man, the reason is because

all the men I've ever known hate shopping quite a lot;
and would never watch commercials to find out what is hot.

He'd have the lists of children's wants all over the darned house,
jotted down on envelopes, then be angry with his spouse

for moving them or losing them, and he could never find
half of all the presents...and they'd get left behind.

He'd have to ask directions so he'd not lose his way,
or have the missus go along to back-seat drive his sleigh.

Why, even Lewis & Clark, who we honor yet today,
had to get a woman to guide them on their way.

And did you ever meet a man who'd wear a suit of red
trimmed in fur all fluffy, that dumb hat upon his head?

Virginia, please don't take me wrong, he's been real good to me;
but I'm convinced he's not a man...that Santa is a she!

This is in the log house we built in the late 1930's where we lived in the Willamette Valley of Oregon. We moved in during the spring of 1939 when I was ready to graduate from 8th grade. This picture is my family when my husband Vernon and I went to visit one year after we were married. Music was a big part of our lives, and still is, and of course was a big part of how we celebrated holidays.

My two older brothers and my dad drug all the logs down with a team of mules and one horse. My mom and I did a lot of the peeling of the logs after they fell the trees. Mom would make lunch to take up there. We lived a half mile from the site. She made homemade potato chips and I can almost still taste them. Bull Creek ran year 'round just a little ways from the front of the house. There was a spring up on the hill behind the house. Dad and the boys dug a 4x8 foot deep reservoir to hold the water, then they put pipes in to siphon that spring water down into the house, so we had running water in the house. It was 16 years later when they put electricity in that house. What memories!

Syble J. Tomlin Brown; Faith, South Dakota

# THE BEST GIFT I'VE HAD IN YEARS

When your married to a rancher and your income's all from cattle,
you have to cut expenses, 'cause saving's half the battle.

The one thing we cut years ago was gifts for one another;
with kids to raise and bills to pay there was no extra for each other.

But, last year I was a bit surprised when hubby said: "My dear,
the cattle market's up a bit . . . how 'bout a gift this year."

He said to drop a hint or two for what I'd like to have
'cause he was going into Winner to buy some grain for calves.

Now, Main Street there in Winner is only three blocks long
and it don't take long to shop there, 'cause most the stores are gone.

But there's a jewelry store on Main Street with rings of every kind,
and I'd seen one in the window that's imprinted on my mind.

So I told him he would see it in a window of a store
on a corner there on Main Street, and I hinted even more.

"It's round, and it is shiny, and I've wanted one for ages,
and this one is on 'special' and won't take a whole month's wages."

I told him it was silver 'cause he's a little color-blind,
and, "I sure don't need a big one, if it's small I will not mind."

I knew that it'd be special as tears welled in my eyes;
I could hardly wait 'till Christmas to get my special prize.

And imagine my excitement when Christmas finally come;
no gift from him for twenty years and he finally bought me one!

Before he went to get the gift, he said to me, "My Dear,
it was more than I intended to spend on you this year,

but I know how bad you wanted it; you deserve the best one, hon.
They had 'em in three sizes. . . I splurged and bought the biggest one.

And I sure do want to thank you for describing it to me,
it was right there in the window, just like you said it'd be."

Then he went to get the gift, and imagine if you can
how shocked I was when here he came with a great big dog food pan!

He went right on explaining as my jaw had hit the floor
that it was right there in the window of the corner hardware store.

It was silver and was shiny, was nice sized and was round
and he knew I always got upset with the dog eating off the ground.

He said I looked a bit surprised, and asked me, "Why the tears?"
I told him they were happy ones . . . the best gift I've had in years!

# THE ANNUAL CHRISTMAS PROGRAM
*(at a one-room country school)*

Some like a Broadway musical, or an evening at the pops,
while others go to Nashville and to them it is the tops.

But one thing I'll assure you that's much better as a rule,
it's the annual Christmas program at a one-room country school.

They haul out all the little desks and put 'em in a shed,
a stage is made of curtains sewn from sheets off teacher's bed.

The kids make all the trimmings for school and for the tree,
and display their finest artwork for everyone to see.

Then comes that special evening we've all been waiting for;
folding chairs and benches cover up the hardwood floor.

Every kid has learned their parts, they've worked for many days
memorizing lines and words to poems and songs and plays.

Of course, they're not professionals like those in Broadway hits
but you'll find no better acting than in all their little skits.

And later, when the program's done, ol' Santa makes a show;
he's sometimes just a "look-a-like" and someone you should know.

The kids, they all exchange their gifts; of course, the homemade kind.
Those gifts don't cost no money, but no one seems to mind.

And then, to top the evening off, we all get quite a treat
. . . homemade Christmas cookies that the moms have brought to eat.

So this year when you're wondering how to celebrate the Yule,
try the Annual Christmas Program at a one-room Country School.

PLEASANT HILL SCHOOL – 1912
Weaver Township; Tripp County, South Dakota

*(L to R) – Edith Beckner, Vera Beckner, Helen Rahn, Winnie
Beckner, Minnie Rahn, Ida Walker, Jennie Beckner, Mary Bigler,
Mrs. Louie Schmidt, teacher; Eugene Walker, LeRoy Drey, Lloyd
Beckner, Clarence Bigler, Ed Assman, and Kenneth Kindred*

# CHRISTMAS SHOPPING WITH A MAN

My mother tried to warn me from experiences she'd had;
'cuz she once went Christmas shopping and she took along my dad.

But I thought that this adventure would be just like a date;
we'd buy some gifts, go out and eat...just me and my old mate.

I never would have asked him, but I really didn't know
how bad that he would hate it or I wouldn't a-made him go.

You can't take back a yesterday...you can't unring a bell;
but I learned that Christmas shopping with a man can be pure hell.

I've seen him sorting cattle through the snow and rain and muck.
and I know he's pulled a zillion calves when some were really stuck;

He's been caught in a blizzard and fought his share of fire;
been bucked off broncs and hurt real bad, and tangled in barbed wire.

I could go on forever telling troubles in his life,
but nothing had prepared him for shopping with his wife.

Every year I've asked him, and every year he'd just stay home;
and even though I'd beg him, I would have to go alone.

This year I put my foot down and the sparks they really flew,
when I told him he should help 'cause they're his kids and grandkids too!

He asked where we were going, so I told him: "to the mall."
He replied: "Just hit the farm store 'cause it would have most all

of anything we'd need to buy," and thought that it would please
the daughter-in-laws to get Carharts with zippers to the knees!

We finally hit a compromise, deciding on Walmart;
we finally found a parking place and grabbed us both a cart.

I told him we just needed one, to tag along with me;
and that was the beginning of my shopping misery.

I won't go into detail; the bad parts I can't say,
but I never had a worst time than trying to shop that day!

He stalled out at the magazines; I grabbed him by the sleeve
'cuz the one that he was lookin' through, you folks would not believe!

He grumbled 'bout the styles of the fashions on the racks;
all the things I liked he didn't, so I put each item back.

And then he saw the lingerie...I thought his eyes had locked,
...he didn't know they made such stuff and he was really shocked!

And it was quite embarrassing, you could hear him everywhere:
"What kind of broad would be caught dead in such skimpy underwear?"

Well, he was 'bout to meet her and it gave him quite a start;
he sure received a dirty look as she put some in her cart!

As we slithered past the hardware, he said his feet were sore
and he wondered how much longer we would be here in this store.

I left him at the lunch stand, for he'd begun to balk,
with several other "tortured" men, where he could sit and talk.

By then I had a headache and decided to concede
that a "Christmas shopping venture" is something we don't need.

So, I put away my cart, then went to get my honey,
and said I thought this year we'd give the kids and grandkids money.

We spent the next half hour in that great big parking lot
a-tryin' to find where we had parked...a place we'd both forgot.

If I live to be a hundred, until the day I drop,
I will never ever ask a man to help me Christmas shop!

Bundled up in front of their claim shack, is the Al Sheppard Family.
Tripp County, South Dakota, homesteaders.

*1914 Winter at the Parchon Place, Tripp County, South Dakota. Note that a nice frame addition has been added to their claim shack. (Incidentally Dr. Parchon was the only medical doctor to live on a homestead and was called out many a cold winter night to assist someone in need).*

# THE PERFECT GIFT

Not everyone's Christmas is merry,
        not everyone's heart's filled with cheer;
perhaps it's because they are missing
        a loved one not with them this year.

It might be a soldier in service,
        or death might have darkened their door;
there's reasons why some folks are lonely
        and something we should not ignore.

It must be real hard to be lonely,
        while others are happy and gay;
while we see the blue skies and sunshine,
        their skies are cloudy and gray.

And it's easy with our lives so busy
        to not take the time to be there
to help lift a burden for others
        and let them know somebody cares.

If you want to do something this Christmas
        to help those who might be alone,
take time from your parties and shopping
        and give them a call on the phone.

Better yet, pay them a visit
        to let them know somebody cares;
for none of us know of tomorrow
        when we may have crosses to bear.

So this year when you go out shopping
        and know someone needing a lift;
just let them know you're thinking of them,
        . . . you'll give them the best kind of gift.

You won't have to spend any money,
        for we know that the best gifts are free.
Take time for the lonely this Christmas,
        it's just how God meant it to be.

*When I was growing up, the relatives spent many Sunday afternoons and holidays together. I attended school in a little one room country school house, and saw many signs of progress, including the first country telephone system, and what an event that was, as was the first rural mail delivery! My father went to town approximately every ten days, in the wagon of course, usually taking grain, butter and eggs to sell and buy needed groceries and supplies, and would get the mail. I had heard much talk of this big event and my father had put up a mail box. At last the big day came. I was posted at the window to watch and hardly knew what to expect. Here came a little covered cart painted red, white and blue, with U.S. on the side and pulled by one horse. The driver was an old gentleman with white whiskers that resembled Santa Claus. We later learned his name was Mr. Rose.*

*Clara Kayton Larsen – my great aunt*

Some of my mother's family (the Kaytons) at a holiday get-together.

# ALL-AMERICAN CHRISTMAS

An all-American Christmas is hard to have today
  with all the foreign imports that are packed in Santa's sleigh.
The toys all come from China, most clothes are from there too;
  it makes me wonder if his elves have anything to do.

The trees all come from Canada, the trimmings from Hong Kong;
  as I read tags where things are from, I'm thinking something's wrong!
The coat I bought for hubby was made in Timbuktu;
  his Wranglers from Korea, and his vest was made there too.

And what was worse, I went to buy the food for Christmas Day;
  the turkeys that I sorted through had come from Uruguay.
The hams, they came from Mexico, the coffee from Brazil;
  that's where all the nuts came from, ...except for Uncle Bill!

There's fruitcake made in Germany, the rum is from there too;
  (perhaps that is the reason why poor Grandpa got the flu).
The lutefisk came from Norway, it smelled like something dead;
  the English made the muffins, the Frenchmen made the bread.

Then I got to thinking that we'd just go out to eat,
  but all the fast-food joints serve the foreign kind of meat.
There's Mexican, Italian, and cafes that are Chinese;
  Greek recipes for goat meat – right in public, if you please.

Everything's from somewhere else, I'll tell you folks, it's sad
  that an all-American Christmas is so hard to be had.
But from these foreign imports, if you'd like to find relief,
  just go down to your grocery store and buy *American Beef!*

# DEAR SANTA

Are you the same dear Santa Claus that used to visit me
and always left a present underneath our Christmas Tree?

You must be getting really old, 'cause I was pretty small,
and many years have come and gone since when you used to call.

I always was so happy when I found out that you ate
those homemade Christmas cookies that I left you on a plate.

And I guess I never told you that I didn't really mind
the doll you left one Christmas was the "second handed" kind.

I never thanked your missus for the pretty dress she wore,
it was nicer than the new ones down at  Putnam's General Store.

But you must'a hit a lottery or somehow struck some gold
'cause you leave a lot more presents now than in the days of old.

I really didn't mind though that you only brought one toy
'cause you brought a lot of happiness to every girl and boy.

Then you suddenly quit coming, it seems like yesterday
and though I really missed you, you just seemed to fade away.

I often think of Christmas and the way it used to be.
Are you the same dear Santa Claus that used to visit me?

# CHRISTMAS GIFTS

The kids nowadays at Christmas
    usually rake in quite a haul;
it seems however long the list,
    that Santa brings it all.

Then parents help ol' Santa out,
    and sometimes search in vain
for G-I Joes, a tanker truck,
    or fine electric train.

Then here comes Christmas morning;
    it is almost like a sin,
'cause gifts that children like the most
    are "boxes" they come in.

# A SENIOR NEW YEAR'S EVE

It was evening at the ranch house, the sun had just gone down;
    he was thinking of the way things used to be.
It wasn't all that long ago, or that's the way it seemed,
    when he was young, the West was wild and free.

That prompted him to thinking 'bout when *he* was wild and free,
    and my, how fast the years have seemed to roll;
and the missus, she has aged a lot, her hair has turned to gray,
    guess the hard work that she's done has took its toll.

But what the heck, it's New Year's Eve, he'll ask her for a date;
    he thinks that this will sure give her a thrill!
So he hollers, *Get yer dress on, and curl up your hair!*
    *There's a band down at McCawley's Bar and Grill!*

She answers, *What you talking about? I think you've slipped a cog!*
    *McCawley's closed a couple years ago!*
*And why the heck would we go out when you can't drive at night?*
    *Before you ask again, the answer's NO!*

So just like every evening, he stretched out in his chair
    then went looking for something on TV;
she did her Bible study, then listened to the news,
    as she too thought of how things used to be.

It was darned near ten o'clock when she woke her snoring spouse,
    and sent him shuffling off toward his bed;
he put his teeth to soaking in a cup there on the stand,
    as she told him what the weatherman had said.

Then reminded him to take his pills and eat a couple prunes,
    and hoped he'd comprehend what he'd been told;
then said, *Happy New Year papa! Some year we'll have that date;*
    *we'll go out and celebrate 'fore we get old!*

# A NEW YEAR DAWNING

With the dawning comes a New Year,
and a farewell to the old
are you ready for what might be around the bend?
Did you tell someone "you're sorry"
that you might have done some wrong?
. . . it is always best to try to make amends.

Did you think to say "I love you"
or to give someone a hug,
or to thank them for the kindly things they do?
You know that life is fragile
and how soon it will be done,
and the next to not be here just might be you.

When you make your resolutions,
don't plan too far ahead,
it is good to live the best you can each day.
As you travel down the road of life
take time to help a friend,
and share a little kindness on the way.

And thank those folks that sacrifice
so we can live each day
in a country that is rich and proud and free.
Be thankful for the glory
of the old Red, White and Blue,
and remember what it means for you and me.

Yes, dawn will bring a New Year,
and leave the old behind;
we will bid adieu just like we've done before.
Are you ready for the future
. . . what might be around the bend,
and prepared for whatever is in store?

# HALLOWEEN HEADLINES

She had been outside all day repairing fence the calves tore down
when she noticed it was getting late and she must go to town;

the stores would soon be closing and there were several things they'd need
to get them through the next few days, like groceries, salt and feed.

The fall work's always heavy, with round-up and the weaning;
so unexpected torn-down fence gives "work" an extra meaning.

And when you are so busy, you sometimes fail to see
what day it is, or check the time, or where you need to be.

She'd been outside since daylight, with no time to comb her hair;
and the carharts that she wore for work received a brand-new tear.

They were stained with grease and oil from the tractor that she drove,
and some burn holes on the sleeves from the branding-iron stove.

She always wore her carharts when she had to help the men,
so there's bloodstains and manure from the cattle working pen.

She headed into town to get supplies, then hurried back,
unloaded all the feed and salt and every grocery sack.

The next day wasn't near so bad, until the paper came;
the first thing that she noticed was her picture and her name.

Right there on the front page of the local town's Gazette
was the headlines and the picture that she never will forget.

It was of her and her straggly hair and dirty old carharts
putting sacks into her truck from loaded grocery carts.

The title 'neath the photo of this awful shocking scene
was:  "The Annual Costume Winner!"  ...yesterday was Halloween.

*Patchwork on
the Prairie*

Sarah Ellen (Loy) Carr-Smiley "Grandma Smiley" 1863 – 1951

*Sarah was born in Washington, Iowa, the third child of William and Naomi Loy. On February 7, 1881, she married William Carr, and came with him to Nebraska, as a young bride. They farmed in Burt County, near Lyons, for a number of years. While there, they raised three children, Archie, Jessie, and my grandmother, Amy. They eventually moved to a farm near Cope, Colorado, and it was there that her beloved husband, Will, died. In 1934, she married an old friend, Willis J. Smiley of Iowa. After his passing, she moved to Gordon, Nebraska, where she resided with my Grandmother, Amy Kayton, until her death in 1951. She endured the many hardships known to those hardy pioneer women, and all the while found pleasure in making beautiful quilts, many of which are still cherished by her descendants.*

# PRAIRIE PATCHWORK

There's a faded, handmade quilt on the sofa in her room,
and she always had it neatly folded there;
and when I'd ask about it, a smile'd come on her face;
it pleased her so to think that I would care.

She'd open it and tell about the making of each block,
and each one had a story of its own.
It was made when she was young and was living on the ranch
in a sod house that she called her "prairie home."

It was made from scraps of fabric from feedsacks she had saved,
or from worn-out clothes her children had outgrown;
and every single block in that pretty patchwork quilt
just seemed to fit together like a poem.

The pink block was the color of the early morning dawn,
and that crimson one like sumac in the fall;
yellow was the color of her roses by the gate,
and lilac was her favorite one of all.

The dark one made her think about those dry depression years
when all the hills were parched and dusty brown.
Gray was like the rain that fell the day her husband died,
. . . it was after that she had to move to town.

She said that life itself is like a patchwork quilt,
of births and deaths and all things in between;
and just when you are thinking that everything is fine,
along comes something new and unforeseen.

Just like her personal diary, as if she'd written in a book,
with the dawning and the passing of each year;
it seems her hopes and sorrows were recorded in each stitch
and each time that I read it brought a tear.

The story of her life, she said, was stitched in that old quilt;
on a corner on the back she signed her name;
then called it "Prairie Patchwork" . . . she wrote that on there too,
as a tribute to her life there on the plain.

*Mary Sachtjen and Marie (daughter of Frank and Ida Sachtjen) – 1919*
*(The Sachtjens are neighbors to the North of our ranch in*
*Tripp County, South Dakota)*

# GRANDMA'S HOMEMADE APRONS

I remember Grandma,
 and I guess I always will;
I remember how she welcomed me
 to her house up on the hill.

Her homemade pies and cookies
 were the best I've ever ate
and I loved her pansy garden,
 and the roses by her gate.

But the one thing I remember most
 about those days of yore,
was the homemade cotton aprons
 that my Grandma always wore.

All the grandmas wore them;
 whether slender gals or fat;
those aprons kept their dresses clean
 but they were more than that.

They always had a pocket,
 where she kept her handkerchief,
and peppermints for grandkids;
 and she'd wipe our little cheeks

with the tail of that old apron
 when a tear would happen by
from a fall or from a skinned up knee,
 things that'd make a young one cry.

She'd gather up the ends of it,
 and use it for a bag
when picking garden produce,
 even use it for a rag.

She made her pretty aprons
 from feed sacks she had picked
when buying special chicken feed
 and starter for her chicks.

What happened to those aprons?
 No one wears them any more;
those homemade cotton aprons
 that our grandmas always wore.

*My great-aunt, Frances Kayton Hookstra, going to pick berries
along the Platte River near their Butler County farm.
Frances was one of the finest quilters in our family.*

# THE THIMBLE

I found a pretty thimble in a box down in a drawer
and knew at once it was the one my mother always wore.
She cherished that old thimble almost like her wedding band.
Remember how she always seemed to have it on her hand?

She always had some patching in a basket by her chair,
and when she had a moment you would find her working there;
and always, in the evening, by a frame her papa built
you would find her with that thimble, a-stitchin' on a quilt.

She used to tell a story about stirring up some broth;
forgot about that thimble 'till it suddenly came off
and landed in the kettle with the noodles, steaming hot;
then she had to use a ladle to retrieve it from the pot.

If it wasn't on her finger, while doing household chores,
it might be in the pocket of the apron that she wore;
and sometimes when we'd stay inside on cold or rainy days
she'd let us "hide the thimble," 'twas a favorite game we'd play.

Now,  you may think it strange that this simple little thimble
could ever be so special, but to me it is a symbol
of another place in time, and it stirs my memory
as I recall the bygone days and how things used to be.

# NANNY NEEDED

I'd like to find a nanny that would live here in our home
to take care of my hubby 'cause he hates to be alone.
She needs to be a real good cook, and like to clean the house,
to sit and watch the channels roll, and play cards with my spouse.

He's been feeling quite neglected since I learned how to quilt
and the way he pouts around here makes me overwhelmed with guilt.
Furthermore, I just don't like to clean and cook no more;
so I'd like to find a nanny because that's what they are for.

I only have one problem with this quest, so I am told;
see, most of them are young and I would like one that is old.
It'd be nice if she was ugly and okay if she was fat;
A young one that's good looking?  I sure would not want that!

It'd be great if she liked mending because my mending's way behind,
and if she'd do the ironing I really wouldn't mind.
She needs to care for all my plants, I hate to see them wilt;
but I don't want her ever learning how to make a quilt.

'Cause that's what happened to the one I hired once before;
and when she learned to quilt she went a walking out the door.
And I can't do much quilting 'till this vacancy is filled;
the old one is too busy...she's the leader of our guild!

*Quilts were often used as a backdrop for early day photos.
Here is Mary Sachtjen and her two daughters in front of
their rural Tripp County, South Dakota, home.*

# QUILTERS' PARADISE

In these days of mass confusion, dreams of false hope and illusion
    there's an never-ending search for better life.
So I dreamed up an idea, and I'll kinder put it to you
    'bout a safe-house called a Quilters' Paradise.

We will live there quite tribunal in a style of life communal,
    where all we have to do is quilt all day.
There'll be no duties for the women, no cooking or no cleaning,
    where not a bit of work gets in our way.

There will be some cleaning ladies and a day care for the babies
    and we'll all have private rooms in dormitories;
and a rec hall for the hubbies full of TV's and hot tubbies
    where they can all hang out and tell their stories.

But the best thing of it all will be a great big Quilters' Hall
    where there you'll meet your friends and quilt all day.
There'll be lots of quilting tables and a snack bar stocked with bagels
    and what a place to quilt the time away!

But there's just one minor problem that will need a little solving,
    it's the task we'll have of financing this dream;
if one could win a lottery the problem would be solved, you see
    but that will never happen, so it seems.

So the next best resolution that might be the right solution
    would be to start a new religious rite.
We could get a TV program full of patchwork and devotion
    and solicit funding for this quilters' site.

And those of you that's teaching could surely take up preaching
    performing miracles before our eyes!
With the money we could raise, we'd join hands and then give praise
    as our dream comes true of a Quilters' Paradise!

*My grandmother's little rocking chair has been passed down through the generations and now belongs to my niece, Debbie Thompson of Gordon, Nebraska. I wrote this poem about the chair.*

## GRANDMA'S ROCKING CHAIR

There's a little wooden rocker, and as I see it there
a lot of special memories come springing from that chair.

I can see my grandma sitting in her rocker all brand new,
in her pretty eyelet pinafore and high topped button shoes.

And then comes my dear mama, as a toddler sitting there;
I know no sweeter toddler ever rocked in that old chair.

It was used by your own mother, by her sisters, and by you;
and I'll bet your little boy spent some time in that chair too.

That little rocker's precious, so give it special care;
and remember these fond memories of Grandma's rocking chair.

This is me many years ago in my Grandma's rocking chair.

*Without a doubt, Grace Snyder, a Nebraska Sandhills ranch wife, is one of the most famous quilters in America, if not the world. Her quilts won international awards and were made at a time when she was extremely busy and at a time when supplies and money were not plentifull. Here is Grace with one of her most famous quilts, called "Flower Basket Petit Point" which contains approximately 85,875 pieces, and was made over a period of 16 months in 1942 and 1943. The pieces are so small that four squares (eight half-squares) make a block about the size of a postage stamp.*

*Sometimes now, in summer, I go to stand in the old yard. Above me, the cottonwoods grieve under every light breeze that stirs their leaves, and it seems to me that I can see the old house and all of us as we used to be. Such busy years, when I baked our bread, churned our butter, raised a big garden and canned all our vegetables, cured our meat, made all the girls' clothes on the sewing machine I had bought with the orphan calf, helped in the hayfield, and still found a little spare time for piecing quilts.*

Grace Snyder 1882-1982
(excerpt from her biography *No Time on My Hands,*
edited by her daughter, Nellie Snyder Yost)

Grace Snyder raking hay on their Nebraska Sandhills ranch

Grace was always taking care of a bum lamb or orphan calf,
in addition to all her other duties as a housewife, mother,
and helpmate to her rancher husband.

*At the age of 16, Jane Hellyer married Robert Steele Kayton on August 6, 1877. Robert's first wife, Rebecca, had died in childbirth three years earlier, leaving him with five motherless children. After their marriage, Jane gave birth to eight more children, and in spite of the many hardships known to pioneer women, she raised all thirteen children and managed to make many beautiful quilts. (Robert Steele Kayton and his first wife, Rebecca, are my great-great grandparents on my mother's side).*

Jane Hellyer Kayton

Chester and Kenneth Kayton – 1922  - sitting on one of the beautiful quilts made by their grandmother, Jane Hellyer Kayton

# PATCHWORK OF THE PRAIRIE

She called it "patchwork of the prairie"
    and I never understood
how one who had so little
    could make quilts that looked so good.

She used a lot of tiny scraps,
    and wasted not one thing;
just tiny pieces of the past
    to form a Wedding Ring,

Dresden Plate or Sawtooth Star,
    the list went on and on
of quilts she pieced by oil light
    'till all her scraps were gone.

She lived there on a homestead
    on the South Dakota plain;
it was there in her old soddy
    that she stitched away the pain

of hardships only known to those
    who came to pave the way
so we could have the kind of life
    we all enjoy today.

She said she loved the prairie
    and the years of living there;
it was where she raised her family
    and her prairie home was where

she made those lovely patchwork quilts
    and they will always be
more than Patchwork of the Prairie
    'cause they're my grandma's legacy.

*A few years back, the Smithsonian Institution gave the patterns of pioneer quilts endowed to them, to the Chinese Government for reproduction. They, in turn, sell these quilts in America for less money than American quilters can purchase fabrics to make quilts out of. Needless to say, the American quilters were up in arms! (There is nothing like a woman's scorn) They marched on Washington, bombarded their senators, and got the gift of patterns stopped, however, the damage was done. Here's my solution:*

# ODE TO SMITHSONIAN

My friend Mary and I were looking around
    in Walmart in Norfolk one day,
when a light started flashing and over the speaker
    we heard a screechy-voiced lady say:

"There's a blue-light special in the housewares department,
    the imported quilts are real cheap!"
Well, we laid some rubber a-turning our carts
    and we found them stacked up in a heap.

Well, there were some doozies, I picked out a couple
    and Mary, she found three or four;
we paid thirty-eight dollars apiece for them hummers
    and left, quilts in arm, out the door.

But reality struck when we headed outside
    to her van, which we started to pack.
What on earth would we do with those imported quilts?
    They're on sale, and we can't take 'em back.

We certainly can't take them to our next quilt guild meeting.
    Our hearts became heavy with guilt.
Why, we'd rather be caught with some illegal drugs
    than be caught with an imported quilt!

By the time we got home, our juices were flowing
  . . . our creative juices, you know.
I started to cut all those quilts all to pieces
  and Mary? She started to sew.

The first thing we made was a nice little jacket,
    the next thing we made was a vest;
and then a heart necklace, a nice little bag;
    it was fun cutting up all the rest.

Now there's no way on earth I could cut up a quilt
    made by our dear pioneers;
but you give me one of those cheap reproductions
    and I go berserk with a sharp pair of shears!

So the next time you see a special on quilts,
    the kind made in China, you see;
just buy you a couple and get out your shears,
    . . . you'll find what fun crafting can be.

And we'll rid this whole nation of those imported quilts,
    we'll empty the shelves, one by one;
and have us a "challenge" making new things,
    called: "The Ode to Smithsonian!"

# OUR GUILD'S NEXT QUILT SHOW

He sits all alone in his old easy chair;
a-flippin' the channels; his wife is not there.

She's gone to a "quilting" like she does every day;
...it seems anymore that he's just in the way.

His old shirt needs patching; there's a button that's gone;
he once had good meals, now it's food bought from Schwann.

The house is a-clutter, there's cloth everywhere;
. . . on top of the table, on all of the chairs.

There should be a shelter for our men and their pals
ignored and neglected by their needle-pokin' gals.

They could start a "support group" and all they would need
is a TV, remote, and an occasional feed.

I have an idea that will relieve all our guilt!
We'll have all the guilds make some nice raffle quilts,

and sell lots of chances and take all the money
for a nice "half-way house" made especially for honeys

of all of us quilters, and there they could go
with a big screen TV for their rotten old shows;

and there have companions with those other guys,
...the husbands of quilters, now that would be wise!

It would be a big building so there'd be room for them all,
with even a golf course and a great big mess hall.

It would be so darned nice that us ladies would go
there to hang up our quilts for our guild's next quilt show!

# HER FEET WOULD ROCK A CRADLE

Her days were long and lonely when they settled on the range
on a new and virgin homestead out where everything was strange.
She'd left her home in Iowa to come with him out West
and she had to do without so much, but did her level best.

Not any other woman lived for many miles around;
the only view she had was of the rolling prairie ground.
But while her man would toil as the barns and sheds were built,
her feet would rock a cradle while her hands would piece a quilt.

She claimed it was her sanity and pleasing to create
the pretty blocks of patchwork during hours she would wait
for him to ride the ranges, and would watch 'till he'd come home
from a window of their cabin that was built from blocks of loam.

Then in evening after supper, by a lantern burning low,
he would read her favorite stories from the Bible she loved so.
She would piece a "Jacobs Ladder" or a "Star" by oil lights
and would sew them into blankets for the cold Dakota nights.

Now the quilts are worn and faded and are packed in her old chest,
along with other trinkets . . . she has put them all to rest.
There's photographs of loved ones and of friends she used to know,
the little shoes her babies wore, and the Bible she loved so.

Once more her days are lonely with the children grown and gone
and it's been so many years now since her husband has passed on.
Her mind goes back to days gone by; she wanders without guilt,
when her feet would rock a cradle while her hands would piece a quilt.

# THE CHRISTMAS QUILT

The first time that I saw it I was probably five years old.
   In fact, I don't remember it, but that's what I've been told.
My grandma started piecing it some time 'fore I was born,
   and always got it out to show us all on Christmas morn.

You might call it a tradition just within our family;
   each year she'd take it from the trunk for all of us to see.
She'd tell us 'bout each little star that centered every block,
   and how she sewed them all together to form the pretty top.

She told us that the first block was made one winter night
   while thinking 'bout her sailor-boy. . . her heart was filled with fright.
T'was late on Christmas Eve. . .she was lonely as could be;
   he was half-way 'round the world on a ship on foreign sea.

Then thoughts came of another boy that was born that very night;
   and pointing to his birthplace was a great star shining bright.
He was born there in a stable to save us all from sin;
   she prayed he'd bless her sailor-son and please watch over him.

She took a scrap of fabric from her boy's favorite shirt
   and cut a star-shaped pattern, and then she went to work.
She made the first of many blocks that very Christmas eve;
   it gave her peace to sew the stars from scraps of memories.

There were prints from mama's dresses and some from grandpa's clothes
   while others came from feedsacks she'd been saving, I suppose.
A little blue checked star was from a tiny baby dress;
   it died so many years ago . . . her favorite I would guess.

When she got the blocks completed she had made just forty-eight,
   the same as those upon the flag of our United States.
The hours she spent a-quilting it helped pass her time alone
   while waiting for her sailor-son to make it safely home.

She put a label on the back and packed the quilt away;
    she'd give it to her fine young lad when he returned one day.
The label said: "This Quilt was made for Christmas '41;
    'twas made with love to let you know I'm proud you are my son."

Then came that awful message that her son would not come back;
    his ship was at the harbor when the Japanese attacked.
The quilt was left in her old trunk, along with several more,
    a folded flag, a purple heart, and clippings of the war.

It was exactly ten years later, Christmas morning, '51,
    the first time that she showed us all the quilt she'd made her son.
She told us all the story about each and every block
    she'd stitched a lot of memories there in every piece of cloth.

Now, many years have come and gone and Grandma's with her son,
    my granddad, and her baby; her life on earth is done.
I think of that first Christmas and that gift for you and me,
    and like so many soldier boys, Christ died to set us free.

I think of those who died for us and rest beneath the sod
    so we can live in freedom in one nation, under God
and forgetting all those sacrifices sometimes brings me guilt
    but I always am reminded when I see her Christmas Quilt.

# About the Author

Yvonne Hollenbeck lives near the tiny village of Clearfield, in South Central South Dakota, where she and her husband, Glen, own and operate a working cattle and quarter horse ranch. Yvonne actively participates in the every day work involved with the operation of the ranch, and her poetry is a reflection of the experiences gained from being a rancher's wife. An occasional event or memory may also stir her creativity.

Her poetry, often humorous in nature, is based upon her everyday experience, however, she also writes about the not-so-humorous situations her mother and grandmothers experiences in their rural settings. Yvonne is the daughter of a National Champion Old-Time Fiddler, Harry Hanson of Gordon, Nebraska, and great-granddaughter of the well publicized old-time cowboy and frontiersman, Ben Arnold. For a number of years, Yvonne was a professional rodeo organist (where she met her rodeo cowboy and pickup-man husband). She is an award winning quilter and is fast becoming one of the most published cowgirl poets in the West.

Yvonne performs at many public functions throughout the Great Plains and has been featured at many of the top cowboy poetry gatherings in America. She has made four recordings of her poetry, and published two books. Yvonne was the first poet to win both the humorous and serious divisions at the World's only Cowboy Poetry Rodeo held in conjunction with the Western Legends Roundup at Kanab, Utah, only to return the following year to repeat that feat in the silver buckle category. In 2005, she was named the Female Poet of the Year by the Academy of Western Artists, however, her greatest reward is the many friends she has gathered along the way and the many great artists she has had an opportunity to perform with.